Question Bank in Home Science

ABOUT THE AUTHOR

Dr. P. Nazni is Doctorate in Food Science and Nutrition and working as Professor and Head in the Department of Nutrition and Dietetics, Periyar University, Salem, Tamilnadu, India. She proved her knowledge in Nutrition and Dietetics by securing Distinction from Graduation to Doctorate Degree. She is having more than 18 years of teaching and research experience and served in various administrative positions like Syndicate member, Periyar University, Salem and President of International Institute of Food and Nutritional Sciences (IIFANS). Recipient of various awards such as Young Women scientist in Nutrition 2017 by Pearl Foundation, IMRF Best Scientist Award in Clinical Nutrition and Dietetics -2017 sponsored by International Multidisciplinary Research Foundation, Vijayawada, A.P, Outstanding Scientist Award-2016, sponsored by Venus International Foundation, Chennai, Dr. APJ. Abdul Kalam Award for Scientific Excellence 2015, Sponsored by Marina Labs Research and Development, Chennai, Tamilnadu, Young Women Scientist Award (2011), Sponsored by Science city, Govt. of Tamilnadu, Chennai, Young Scientist Fellowship Award (YSFA), Sponsored by TNSCST, Chennai, Tamilnadu, India for 2007-2008, Fellow Award 2010, Sponsored by Society for Applied Biotechnology, Krishnagiri, Tamilnadu, India, 2010, Young Investigator Award, 2011, Sponsored by International College of Nutrition, Canada and Award of Honor, 2012, Sponsored by ICMR & ISSRF on Centenary Celebrations of ICMR. She has presented more than 210 research papers in various National and International Seminars/ Conferences and has published 94 research papers in referred National and International journals. She has been a resource person and delivered invited talks in 122 seminars/conference/workshops both national and international. She has visited various countries like Canada, Australia, South Africa, Czech Republic, Thailand, UAE and Iran for her invited talks and paper presentations. She has organized around 43 National and International conferences in various capacities. She has completed Five Major research projects funded by UGC, DST, RSSDI and ICMR and 11 Minor research projects and currently working with four major projects with the worth of Rs.1.7 crores. She has written seven books published by various reputed publications. She has guided 66 M.Sc, 48 M.Phil and 11 Ph. D candidates with 8 Ph.D students under guidance. She has been Editorial board member in various reputed Food science and Nutrition journal's. She is a Managing Editor of an International Journal of Food and Nutritional Sciences, published by IIFANS. She is also having membership in various Professional Bodies such as Indian Dietetic Association (IDA) (Life Member), Indian Academy of Social Sciences (Life Member), Nutrition Society of India (NSI), Food Security Community (Life Member) and Association of Food Scientists and Technologists in India (AFSTI) (Full Member).

Question Bank in Home Science

P. Nazni
Professor & Head
Department of Nutrition and Dietetics
Periyar University, Salem, Tamilnadu

A Paperback Division of

NEW INDIA PUBLISHING AGENCY

101, Vikas Surya Plaza, CU Block, LSC Market
Pitam Pura, New Delhi 110 034, India
Phone: + 91 (11)27 34 17 17 Fax: + 91(11) 27 34 16 16
Email: info@nipabooks.com
Web: www.nipabooks.com

Feedback at feedbacks@nipabooks.com

ISBN No. 978-93-87973-12-1

Composed, Designed & Printed in India

Preface

Home science is a scientific course of study which moulds a student with a variety of life skills. This is a unique discipline with a blend of science and art. It does not limit itself to the home related skills of cooking, laundry, decoration and stitching. Home science is now out of the shell of misconceptions and opened its doors for new avenues in all possible fields of life. This is a recognised professional course and requires its students to have a logical and intellectual mind. As there is a growing concern for health and nutrition, the changing lifestyle of present generation, Home Science course has come to limelight. Its changing outlook has attracted several students enabling them to pursue a successful career.

In the last decade, many Indian educational organizations including university departments, institutions, colleges and deemed universities have started undergraduate, postgraduate and doctorate degree programmes related to Home science and its disciplinary subjects. Many of these institutes conduct entrance examination for admission in these courses. Apart from that, some national level examinations such as UGC-NET and SLET will be conducted every year in the area of Home Science. Hence there is a great need of an objective type book covering all important topics of subjects related to Home Science. Hence, this book is written to compensate the demand of students and to help them in making their career in the areas of Home Science.

This book includes the objective information of the subjects such as Food Science, Nutrition Science, Textile and Clothing, Family Resource Management, Human Development, Food Service Management, Extension Education and Research Methodology. This book can serve as a single platform for preparation of competitive examinations in Home Science Discipline. We wish to acknowledge the authors and editors of all the reference books and research publications which helped us in the preparation of this book. I wish to thank the Almighty for his blessings and also to my research scholars for their inspiration and support in completing this book. Last but not least I must thank my family for their love, support and encouragement.

P. Nazni

Contents

1

Food Science

1. Food exchange lists include
   a) Milk list b) Meat list
   c) Bread list d) All the above
2. Which food group occupies the tip of the food pyramid
   a) Fats, oil and sugar b) Milk and pulses
   c) Vegetables and fruits d) Cereals and millets
3. According to ICMR foods have been classified into _______ groups.
   a) Six groups b) Five groups
   c) Four groups d) Seven groups
4. Which food group forms the base of the food pyramid
   a) Cereals b) Vegetables and fruits
   c) Milk and meat d) Pulses
5. _________ produces aflatoxins in groundnuts.
   a) Clostridium botulism b) Aspergillus flavus
   c) Salmonella d) Streptococci
6. Fruits and vegetables are
   a) Protective foods b) Energy giving foods
   c) Body building foods d) All the above
7. Which is incorrectly matched
   a) Energy giving food-rice b) Body building food-green gram
   c) Protective foods-spinach d) Regulatory food-fat
8. Food is cooked uncovered on heated metal or frying pan the method is known as __________.
   a) Baking b) Sautéing
   c) Pan broiling d) Simmering

9. A temperature that is maintained inside the oven is ________.
   a) 160°C – 200°C b) 200°C – 250°C
   c) 120°C – 260°C d) 180°C – 240°C
10. Ragi is a rich source of ________
    a) Calcium and iron b) Sodium and Phosphorous
    c) Magnesium and Manganese d) Folic acid and vitamin B_{12}.
11. Oils extracted from the cereal grains contain high amount of ________.
    a) Vitamin B_1 b) Vitamin B_2
    c) Vitamin E d) Vitamin A
12. Presence of ________ gives aroma to Rice.
    a) Acetyl 1-1 pyruvate b) Acetyl 1-2 pyrroline
    c) Acetyl 1-6 pyrroline d) 2- Acetyl- 1- pyrroline
13. ARF stands for ________.
    a) Aminoacid Rich food b) Amylase Rich food
    c) Amylose Rich food d) Acid Rich food
14. Familiae compound of glutamic acid derived from wheat is ________.
    a) Di Sodium Glutamate b) Mono sodium glutamate
    c) Sodium Glutamate d) Tri sodium Glutamate.
15. ________ is a hybrid cereal from a cross between wheat and rye.
    a) Triticum b) Secale
    c) Tritical d) Triticate
16. In Rice, alkaline is present in the form of ________.
    a) Albumin b) Globulin
    c) Prolamines d) Oryzenin
17. The protein present in rice consists of the biological value of ________.
    a) 66% b) 50 %
    c) 80 % d) 85%
18. ________ in fresh rice is probably responsible for its sticky consistency after cooking
    a) Alpha amylase b) Beta amylase
    c) Amylose d) Peroxidases

19. ________ is the process of plunging food into boiling liquid and immersing in cold water.

a) Fermentation b) Marinating

c) Blanching d) Stringing

20. ________ can be added for variety in the diet.

a) Arhar b) Urad

c) Soya nuggets d) Rajmah

21. Pearl millet is called as ________

a) Finger millet b) Jowar

c) Bajra d) Maize

22. Which of the following is rich in phosphorous

a) Carbohydrate b) Fats

c) Nucleic acids d) Proteins

23. The unavailable sugar in pulses includes ________ which produce flatulence in man.

a) Mono Saccharides and Mannose

b) Di Saccharides and Cellulose

c) Oligo Saccharides and raffinose

d) Poly Saccharides and hemi cellulose

24. Legume seeds are rich in ________.

a) Vitamin B b) Vitamin A

c) Vitamin C d) Vitamin K

25. Tempeh is fermented by ________.

a) MicroCoccus b) Bacillus

c) Rhizopus Oligoporous d) Rhizopusbulgaricus

26. Soy Sauce is fermented by ________.

a) Rhizopus oligoposrous b) Bacillus subtilis

c) Aspergillus oryzae d) Micro cocci

27. Cow's milk contains ______ percent of fat.

a) 4.1 b) 3.1

c) 5.3 d) 6.1

28. __________ are responsible for the yellow colour of milk fat Casein.

a) Carotenes b) Casein

c) Flavanoids d) Flavins

29. Fresh milk has a pH of about __________ percent.

a) 6.4-6.5 b) 6.5-6.7

c) 6.7-6.8 d) 6.3-6.6

30. Milk is a rich source of __________

a) Vitamin A b) Vitamin D

c) Vitamin C d) Vitamin K

31. Lactoglobulin is present in __________.

a) Mineral mix b) Vitamin mix

c) Whey protein d) None of the above

32. In milk brown colour is formed due to __________.

a) Heating b) Scorching

c) Oxidation d) Maillard reaction

33. A balanced diet is the one which is__________.

a) Tasty b) Nutritious

c) Appealing d) Easy to prepare

34. Fruits and vegetables are rich in

a) Carbohydrates b) Vitamins

c) Both a and b d) Fats

35. Best protein choices are

a) Fish b) Poultry

c) Both a and b d) Pizza

36. Which nutrient makes up most of your body?

a) Vitamins b) Minerals

c) Protein d) Carbon

37. Which food group forms major portion of your diet each day?

a) Vegetables b) Grains

c) Fruits d) Nuts

38. Which nutrient helps you grow and build strong muscles?

a) Protein b) Energy

c) Lipids d) Fibre

39. Strawberry belongs to which food group

a) Vegetables b) Fructose

c) Fruits d) Cereals

40. Which nutrient provides you with first source of energy?

a) Protein b) B-vitamin

c) Fat d) Carbohydrate

41. Which fat is the "healthy" fat?

a) Saturated fat b) Trans fat

c) Animal fat d) Unsaturated fat

42. The best protein can be found mostly in which food group

a) Vegetables b) Grains

c) Meat and beans d) Oil

43. Xanthophylls bring the colour to ________.

a) Egg yolk b) Egg white

c) Egg shell d) Whole egg

44. Fat penetrates between the muscle fibre bundles is known as ________

a) Collagen b) Elastin

c) Marbling d) Myoglobin

45. Tenderizing enzyme present in the fig is ________

a) Papain b) Ficin

c) Bromelain d) None of the above

46. Biological value of fish protein is ________

a) 90 b) 80

c) 75 d) 70

47. Oyster is a poor source of ________

a) Zinc b) Fibre

c) Manganese d) Magnesium

48. One gram of fat gives ________ kilocalories.

a) 4 b) 7

c) 5 d) 9

49. Egg yolk is enclosed by a sac called ________.

a) Chalazae b) Vitelline

c) Both a and b d) None

50. Which of the following cooking methods is not a moi-t heat method?

a) Simmering b) Roasting

c) Steaming d) Poaching

51. The temperature used for deep fat frying is

a) 177-191°C b) 160-180°C

c) 180-220°C d) 220-250°C

52. Cooking of food in a slightly greased pan is

a) Sautéing b) Shallow fat frying

c) Deep fat frying d) Braising

53. Corn flour is used as the ____________agent

a) Stabilizing b) Thickening

c) Emulsifying d) All the above

54. Changes brought to starch granules by dry heat is called

a) Retrogration b) Gelation

c) Dextrinisation d) Gelatinisation

55. Low-acid foods have pH values of ____ or less.

a) 5.2 b) 3.9

c) 4.6 d) 4.2

56. Cool storage is considered any temperature from ____°F to ____°F.

a) 28, 68 b) 28, 78

c) 18, 48 d) 32, 58

57. Household refrigerators usually run at ____°F to ____°F.

a) 45.5, 50.2 b) 32.3, 35.7

c) 40.5, 44.6 d) 21.4, 26.5

58. Intimate contact occurs between the food or package and the refrigerant with ____ freezing.

a) Blast b) Cold
c) Pressure d) Immersion

59. The freezing point for pure water is ____°F.

a) 10 b) 28
c) 15 d) 32

60. How long frozen orange juice can be stored at 10°F?

a) 14 months b) 10 months
c) 6 months d) 2 months

61. Which vitamin is used most commonly to control browning in fruits by enzymes?

a) K b) B
c) C d) D

62. The lower limit of moisture by sun drying is approximately ____ percent.

a) 10 b) 20
c) 30 d) 15

63. Foods high in ____ or other solutes dry more slowly.

a) Protein b) Sugar
c) Salt d) Water

64. ____ is when water goes from a solid to a gas without passing through the liquid phase.

a) Sublimation b) Evaporation
c) Transfusion d) Condensation

65. Reducing the volume and weight of a product saves ____ during processing.

a) Time b) Money
c) energy d) Flavor

66. Low-temperature ____ evaporators are used for heat-sensitive foods.

a) Ultrafiltration b) Vacuum
c) Osmosis d) Drum

67. Sun-dried ____ is the best known of all dried foods.
    a) Tomatoes b) Raisins
    c) Peppers d) Mushrooms
68. To dry fruits out-of-doors, humidity below ____ percent is best.
    a) 60 b) 80
    c) 70 d) 90
69. Which of the following is rich in iron content?
    a) Mint d) Potato
    c) Sweet potato d) Turnip
70. Foods that are sterilized by irradiation can be stored for ____ without refrigeration
    a) Weeks b) Years
    c) Months d) Days
71. Microwave radiation is often called ____ radiation.
    a) Ionizing b) Electrical
    c) Non-ionizing d) Magnetic
72. Irradiation causes undesirable flavor changes in ____ products.
    a) Dairy b) Meat
    c) Grain d) Vegetable
73. In ____, FDA approved the use of irradiation to control pathogens in fresh and frozen red meats, such as beef, lamb, and pork.
    a) 1988 b) 1975
    c) 1997 d) 1990
74. Fish is usually cooked by ______.
    a) Dry heat boiling b) Baking
    c) Frying d) All of the above
75. Fish can be cured by
    a) Pickling b) Salting
    c) Drying d) All the above
76. Salting is done with addition of _______.
    a) Sodium Nitrite b) Sodium bicarbonate
    c) Sodium bisulphate d) None of the above

77. Chlorophyll a is ________ in colour.

a) Blue green
b) Yellow green
c) Green
d) None of the above

78. Pigment present in yellow corn is ________

a) Lycopene
b) Lutein
c) Cryptoxanthin
d) Capsorubin

79. ________ compound is present in raw cabbage.

a) S – methyl-L- cysteine sulphoxide
b) S – methyl-L - cysteine
c) S – methyl-L- cysteine sulphur oxide
d) S– methyl-L- cysteine sulphur dioxide

80. __________ added to the cooking water disintegrates the hemi cellulose and cellulose.

a) Sodium carbonate
b) Sodium bicarbonate
c) Sodium benzoate
d) None of these

81. MAP stands for __________.

a) Modified Atmosphere Packaging
b) Medium Atmosphere Packaging
c) Moderate Atmosphere Packaging
d) Moderate Air Packaging

82. Mushroom belongs to ________.

a) Fungi
b) Algae
c) Bacteria
d) Virus

83. Mushroom contains __________ percent of protein.

a) 10-20
b) 20-30
c) 20-40
d) 20-25

84. Avocado is rich in ________

a) Carbohydrate
b) Fat
c) Protein
d) Vitamin

85. Lycopene is rich in ______ .

a) Mango
b) Peaches
c) Plums
d) Grapes

86. _________ pectic substance is present in raw fruits and vegetables.

a) Protopectin b) Pectimic acid

c) Pectin d) Pectic acid

87. The other name for invertase is ______.

a) Sucrose b) Maltose

c) Lactose d) Galactose

88. In _________ temperature caramelization of fructose takes place.

a) 110°C b) 120°C

c) 180°C d) 170°C

89. HFCS stands for ______.

a) High Fructose Corn Syrup b) High Fructose Content Syrup

c) High Fructose Content Sample d) None of these.

90. Honey contains ________ of water.

a) 12 % b) 15 %

c) 17 % d) 80 %

91. The colour of the honey is related to ________ content.

a) Vitamins b) Minerals

c) Both a & b d) Proteins

92. Jaggery contains high amount of _______.

a) Calcium b) Potassium

c) Sodium d) Iron

93. Hard ball is obtained at ________ temperature in sugar cookery.

a) 112 – 120°C b) 121 – 130°C

c) 132 – 154°C d) 149 – 154°C

94. Caramel sugar can be prepared from ______.

a) Soya bean b) Tapioca

c) Sago d) None of the these

95. In honey ______ percent of fructose is present.

a) 38 b) 31

c) 7 d) 2

96. Fishe.s can be preserved by

a) Canning b) Chilling
c) Freezing d) All the above

97. The factors affecting storage of vegetables are:

a) Loss of water b) Microorganisms
c) Respiration d) All the above

98. The preservative used in butter is

a) Sodium benzoate b) Sodium carbonate
c) Sodium bicarbonate d) All the above

99. Milk is adulterated by ________.

a) Oil b) Water
c) Both a and b d) None of these

100. Salt and sugar is adulterated by ________.

a) Starch b) Chalk powder
c) White powdered stone d) None of these

101. The preservation of Food Adulteration Act was passed in

a) 1948 b) 1954
c) 1958 d) 1962

102. The preservative used for preserving fishes is

a) Sodium chloride b) Sugar
c) Vinegar d) None of the above

103. Food can be packed in

a) Cans b) Glass jars
c) Cartons d) All the above

104. Acid foods can be processed safely as initial temperature reaches________.

a) 75.2°C b) 82.2°C
c) 71.1°C d) 76.2°C

105. Preservatives added to squash are ________.

a) Citric acid b) Sucrose
c) Sodium benzoate d) All of the above

106. According to FPO "Pickling in salt" sodium chloride should not be less than ______.

a) 10% b) 15%

c) 20% d) 15.5%

107. ________spices contain bacteriostatic effect.

a) Turmeric powder b) Tamarind

c) Chilli powder d) All of these

108. For preserving fruits and vegetables the preservatives used is

a) Sulpur dioxide b) Sodium benzoate

c) Sorbic acid d) Citric acid

109. Sulphurous acid inhibits the growth of

a) Yeasts b) Moulds

c) Bacteria d) All the above

110. Epoxides are highly effective in preservation of

a) Citric acid fruits b) Spices

c) Low moisture foods d) Nuts

111. _____ is an older method of preservation.

a) Drying b) Freezing

c) Irradiation d) None of them

112. In sharp freezing the temperature is maintained at _______.

a) -4°C - 29°C b) 5⁰C-30°C

c) 10°C-15°C d) 3⁰C-15°C

113. Removal of microorganisms can be done by______ process.

a) Asepsis b) Filtration

c) Heat d) Blanching

114. ______ is the designer foods.

a) Nutraceuticals b) Functional foods

c) Pharma foods d) All the above

115. Normal freezing point of milk is ______.

a) -0.55°C b) -0.54°C

c) 0.55°C d) 0.66°C

116. Diethyl pyrocarbonate are used as a preservative for

a) Spices b) Fruits juices

c) Nuts d) Vegetables

117. An excellent stabilizing agent in cakes is

a) Milk b) Egg yolk

c) Cream d) Butter

118. Chilli powder is adulterated by ______.

a) Brick powder b) Soap stone

c) Artificial colour d) All of these

119. Meat or poultry is simmered in water is known as______.

a) Red stock b) Broth

c) Brown stock d) Gumbo

120. Which of the bacteria can grow in alkaline pH?

a) Lactobacilli b) Salmonella

c) Vibrio cholera d) Staphylococcus

121. Fermentation is the ____ form of food preservation.

a) Oldest b) Best

c) Newest d) Cheapest

122. Lactic acid bacteria with propionic acid bacteria produce ____ cheese.

a) Cheddar b) Swiss

c) Mozzarella d) Monterey jack

123. Fermentation microorganisms produce ____ and growth factors in the food.

a) Minerals b) Calories

c) Vitamins d) Energy

124. Fermentation is stopped by pasteurizing and ____.

a) Cooling b) Stirring

c) Heating d) Settling

125. Yogurt is a semi-solid fermented milk product that originated centuries ago in __

a) Hungary b) Romania

c) Central Asia d) Germany

126. Sour cream usually has a fat content between ____ percent.

a) 1 and 2 b) 10 and 11

c) 3 and 8 d) 12 and 30

127. Bread is leavened with ____.

a) Yeast b) Salt

c) Sugar d) Baking soda

128. Vinegar usually has an acetic acid content of between 4 and ____ percent.

a) 6 b) 8

c) 7 d) 9

129. GMO stands for ____.

a) Genetically Modified Organism

b) Gross Moldy Oranges

c) Genetically Manufactured Oranges

d) Genetically Malfunctioning Organisms

130. The use of food additives is controlled by the ____ clause.

a) Delaney b) Delaware

c) Additive d) Supplement

131. ____ is the most heavily used additives.

a) Minerals b) Gums

c) Vitamins d) Sweeteners

132. Sequestrants are ____ agents.

a) Cheating b) Chilling

c) Chelating d) Charcoal

133. In terms of additives, ____ include both natural and synthetic colorants.

a) Flavors b) Colors

c) Gums d) Sweeteners

134. ____ dissolve in water and are made as powders, granules (small hard pieces), liquids, or other special purpose forms.

a) Dyes b) Sweeteners

c) Lakes d) Gums

135. ____ make a food acid or sour.

a) Flavorings b) Colorings

c) Texturing d) Acidulate

136. UPC stands for ____.

a) Universal Packaging Code b) United Product Code

c) United Packaging Code d) Universal Product Code

137. Meat should be packed in ________.

a) Glass bottles b) Polyethylene sheets

c) Plastics d) None

138. The outside of the steel can is protected from rust by a thin layer of ________

a) Tin b) Aluminum

c) Copper d) Silver

139. Drumstick leaves are rich in

a) Calcium b) Potassium

c) Magnesium d) Manganese

140. The red colour in the skin of radish is due to the

a) Flavonoids b) Anthoxanthins

c) Anthocyanins d) All the above

141. Beet root contain a pigment called

a) Anthocyanins b) Betacyanins

c) Betaxanthin d) Both b and c

142. Sinigrin is produced when______ is cooked

a) Cabbage b) Beans

c) Cauliflower d) Lady's finger

143. Which of the following has excellent oxidative stability?

a) Sunflower oil b) Safflower oil

c) Corn oil d) Peanut oil

144. The conversion of liquid oil to solid shortenings is called as

a) Hydrogenation b) Winterization

c) Hydration d) All the above

145. Which of the following is a thickening agent

a) Saffron b) Pepper

c) Tamarind d) Poppy Seeds

146. Clear soups prepared with meat stock are________.

a) Extraction b) Full-flavoured

c) Stimulate the appetite d) All of these

147. BVO stands for________

a) Brominated Vegetable Oil b) Bromin Vegetable Oil

c) Brominated Virgin Oil d) Boviated Virgin Oil

148. Vegetables are used in

a) Curries b) Salads

c) Stuffing d) All the above

149. Safflower oil has ______________linoleic acid

a) 25-50% b) 75-80%

c) 80-90% d) 90-100%

150. Which of the adulterant is commonly present in coffee?

a) Chicory b) Tamarind

c) Dates seed powder d) All of these

151. _____ contains very high shortening value.

a) Coconut oil b) Lard

c) Sunflower oil d) Butter

152. _____ is one of the newest method of heating food.

a) Ohmic heating b) Microwave heating

c) Irradiation d) Ionizing radiation

153. The whole egg contains ____________ percent of water.

a) 60 b) 50

c) 74 d) 66

154. Gelation of egg yolk on freezing is prevented by the addition of________ % sugar.

a) 20% b) 10%

c) 15% d) 25%

155. Protein content of cocoa is______.

a) 20.0% b) 21.5%

c) 22.5% d) 23.1%

156. Total ash content in tea varies from ______

a) 3-5% b) 4-7%

c) 5-6% d) 6-7%

157. Egg yolk is an

a) Emulsifying agent b) Stabilizing agent

c) Hydrogenating agent d) All the above

158. Fat improves the texture of food by acting as

a) Leavening agent b) Shortening agent

c) Smoothening agent d) All the above

159. Turmeric contain ______ of essential oil.

a) 4% b) 5%

c) 7% d) 10%

160. BIS was passed in the year ______.

a) 1986 b) 1985

c) 1987 d) 1988

161. ______ is used to find out the specific gravity in milk.

a) Fractometer b) Lactometer

c) Penetrometer d) Refractometer

162. Sensory evaluation of food should be done in the

a) Morning b) Mid-morning

c) Afternoon d) Evening

163. Measurement of the colour of foods cannot be done by

a) Spectrophotometer b) Centrifugation

c) Tintometer d) Colour dictionaries

164. The methods of drying are

a) Freeze drying b) Spray drying

c) Foam mat drying d) All the above

165. Nuts are used in

a) Chutneys b) Sweets

c) Cakes d) All the above

166. Flour analysis in product containing different taste and odour is evaluated by method_________.

a) Sensitivity threshold test b) Dilution test

c) Descriptive flavor profile d) None of these

167. _________is used to measure butter content in milk.

a) pH b) Refractometer

c) Poloriscope d) Butyrometer

168. ________ is used to measure tenderness of meat.

a) Shear press b) Warner-Bratzler Shear

c) Compressimeter d) Tensile strength

169. The oil extracted from rice bran is rich in __________.

a) Vitamin A b) Vitamin K

c) Vitamin E d) Vitamin C

170Loosing water from gel is called __________________.

a) Retrogradation b) Weeping

c) Syneresis d) All of the above

171. Peeling apples may result in the loss of ______________ of their ascorbic acid.

a) 10-25% b) 8-25%

c) 25-30% d) 5-10%

172. ___________ temperature have an unfavorable effect on the palatability of canned fruits.

a) Low temp b) High temp

c) Medium temp d) Very high temp

173. _______ aromatic compound in pineapple gives flavor.

a) Methyl butyrate b) Aldehydes

c) Terpenes d) Ethyl butyral

174. Egg contains all the nutrients except ______.

a) Avidin b) Carbohydrates

c) Riboflavin d) Biotin

175. Fruits of plum family contain ________ acid.

a) Acetic acid d) Malic acid

c) Citric acid d) Both b and c

176. Benzoic acid cannot be used by the body but excreted as ______ acid.

a) Hippuric acid b) Tartaric acid

c) Malic acid d) Citric acid

177. ________ affects the flavor of fruits.

a) Sugars b) Tannins

c) Minerals salts d) All of these

178. ______________ reacts with metals and brings about undesirable changes.

a) Anthocyanin b) Anthoxanthin

c) Both a and b d) Chlorophyll

179. Citrus fruits should be refrigerated between _________ degree Celsius.

a) 14-20 b) 13-15

c) 15-20 d) 20-25

180. Active principle present in vanilla is ______.

a) Vanellin b Vanillin

c) Venallin d) None of these

181. Garlic and onion inhibit growth of fungi belonging to ______.

a) Aspergillus b) Candida

c) Both a and b d) None of these

182. Addition of _________ strengthens the cell structure.

a) Sugar b) Salt

c) Both a and b d) None of these

183. Which of the following is considered in cooking of fruits?

a) Amount of pectin b) Degree of ripeness

c) Amount of sugar and water d) All of these

184. __________ gives the characteristics of flavor and aroma to fruits.

a) Formic acid b) Caproic acid

c) Both a and b d) None of these

185. Green colour of vegetable is due to __________ pigment.

a) Carotenoids b) Flavonoid

c) Anthocyanin d) Chlorophyll

186. Bitterness in fruits can be attributed to

a) Anthocyanins b) Flavonoids

c) Carotenoids d) Anthoxanthin

187. The colour of the meat is due to __________

a) Albumin b) Globulin

c) Cathepsins d) Myoglobin

188. Pasteurization is a method of preservation using

a) Thermal processing b) Evaporation

c) Irradiation d) Fermentation

189. Cream of tartar and tartaric acid is

a) Fast-acting baking powders b) Slow acting baking powders

c) Combination baking powders d) None of these

190. Platelet aggregation inhibitory factors is possessed by

a) Garlic b) Kokum

c) Saffron d) Onion

191. Infant milk foods in India are fortified with________.

a) Vitamin A b) Vitamin E

c) Vitamin B d) Vitamin D

192. Sugar products are enriched with________.

a) Thiamine b) Niacin

c) Both a and b d) None of these

193. ________ is prepared by fermenting milk of mare.

a) Koumiss b) Kefir

c) Cheese d) None of these

194. Kefir is prepared by fermenting milk of sheep and goat by_______.

a) Lactic acid bacteria b) Yeast

c) Both a and b d) None of these

195. _______is made by fermenting a mixture of soybean and wheat.

a) Lactic soybean curd b) Soybean gheer

c) Soy sauce d) None of these

196. Food spoilage is caused due to_______.

a) Microorganisms b) Insects

c) Enzymes d) All of these

197. _______ is known as monosodium glutamate.

a) Ajinomoto b) Turmeric

c) Vanilla d) Citric acid crystals

198. The temperature of home refrigerates should be maintained at_______.

a) 6°C b) 10°C

c) 12°C d) 15°C

199. In dehydro freezing fruits and vegetable are dried about_______ percentage.

a) 25% b) 50%

c) 30% d) 35%

200. Dehydro freezing is mainly used in_______.

a) Homes b) Institutional food service

c) Both a and b d) None of these

201. Pasteurization is done in_______ foods.

a) Milk b) Juices

c) Cream d) All of these

202. _______ is destroyed at boiling temperature.

a) Yeast b) Mould

c) Enzymes d) All of these

203. Canning is successful if the food keeps without spoilage and the canned food is thus termed as ______.

a) Sterile b) Commercially sterile

c) Both a and b d) None of these

204. Dehydrated food contains only________% moisture.
a) 1-2% b) 2-3%
c) 3-5% d) 5-6%

205. Freeze drying requires________ hours.
a) 10-20 hrs b) 5-10 hrs
c) 10-25 hrs d) 24 hrs

206. In freeze drying moisture content in food is about_______%.
a) 1-4% b) 1-5%
c) 5-10% d) 1-6%

207. Tenderness is improved if the meat is hydrated in a ______% brine solution.
a) 5% b) 2%
c) 3% d) 10%

208. Foam meat drying is used in______ foods.
a) Milk b) Tomato
c) Fruit juice d) All of these

209. Powdered dry foods are dispersed in water then particles are clustered after drying is called as________.
a) Foam meat drying b) Instantizing
c) Explosion d) Reverse osmosis

210. Permitted level and kinds of food additives have been specified by_______.
a) FPO b) PFA
c) AGMARK d) MPO

211. _______ chemical is used to prevent the discoloration of dried fruits.
a) Benzoates b) Sulphur di oxides
c) Potassium sorbates d) Sorbic acid

212. Common sequestrants used in dairy products are________.
a) Sodium salt b) Citric acid
c) Metaphosphoric acid d) All of these

213. Emulsifiers are sometimes called as_______.
a) Surfactants b) Surface active agents
c) Both a and b d) None of these

214. Optimal temperature for drying is ______degree.

a) 52°C b) 60°C

c) 66°C d) 70°C

215. ________is used to determine the pectin content of juices.

a) Jelmeter b) Jar tongs

c) Refractometer d) Penetrometer

216. In hot pack method temperature should be maintained at_______degree.

a) 70°C b) 77°C

c) 78°C d) 80°C

217. Fruit juices are heated at ______degree to kill microbes.

a) 150°C b) 100°C

c) 200°C d) 220°C

218. Which of the following fruits are rich in pectin and low in acid?

a) Figs b) Bananas

c) Sweet apple d) All of these

219. Commercial pectin is prepared from _______.

a) Apples b) Citrus peels

c) Both a and b d) None of these

220. MPO stands for_______.

a) Meat Product Order b) Metro Products Order

c) Milk Product Order d) Milk Producer's Organization

221. MPO is passed in the year______.

a) 1973 b) 1970

c) 1974 d) 1975

222. Which of the following foods are graded under AGMARK?

a) Legumes b) Butter

c) Oil d) All of these

223. Jellies are cooked at ______ temperature.

a) 180°F b) 240°F

c) 300°F d) 220°F

224. Fruits should be cooked for_______ minutes.

a) 10-20 min b) 5-10 min

c) 10-15 min d) 15-20 min

225. Sugar concentration in jelly may vary from_______ %.

a) 40-70% b) 65-69%

c) 50-55% d) 55-75%

226. _______ fruit is usually considered to be low in both acid and pectin.

a) Pears b) Strawberries

c) Guava d) Apple

227. ______ percentage of salt is added to juice.

a) 1 b) 2

c) 2.5 d) 3.5

228. _______ chemical bleaches the colour of coloured fruits.

a) Potassium metabisulphite b) Sodium benzoate

c) Both a and b d) None of these

229. Moulding and pressing of fat in the various shapes without breaking is called______.

a) Hydrogenation b) Plasticity

c) Winterisation d) Emulsification

230. _______ spices is obtained from dried flower bud.

a) Cumin seed b) Clove

c) Cardamom d) Aniseed

231. Which of the following is the role of spices in cookery?

a) Souring agent b) Thickening agent

c) Emulsifier d) All of these

232. Beverages can be classified according to their functions in the body on_______.

a) Nourishing b) Stimulating

c) Soothing d) All of these

233. The main criteria in judging the coffee quality is/are_______.

a) Strength b) Flavour

c) Acidity d) All of these

234. A brine solution is

a) Water and salt solution b) Water and sugar solution

c) Water and soda solution d) Fat and water mixture

235. Which of the following is required for making jams and jellies?

a) Vinegar b) Acids

c) Pectin d) None of the above

236. A processing technique that preserves food by lowering food temperature to the point at which life processes cease is called

a) Canning b) Freezing

c) Drying d) Extrusion

237. Which one of the following is a low-temperature acid salts?

a) Tartaric acid b) Monocalicium phosphate

c) Cream of tartar d) All of the above

238. To prevent food poisoning

a) Leftovers should be transferred to deep refrigerating

b) Perishables should be immediately refrigerated

c) Frozen poultry in thawed in refrigerator

d) Both b and c

239. The protein that is responsible for jelly like character of egg white is

a) Ovalbumin b) Ovomucin

c) Ovomucoid d) Conalbumin

240. Phosvitin is rich in

a) Potassium b) Calcium

c) Phosphorous d) Magnesium

241. Livetin is rich in

a) Sulphur b) Calcium

c) Potassium d) Manganese

242. The amount of energy present in egg per 100g is

a) 150kcal b) 155kcal

c) 185kcal d) 200kcal

243. An average egg contain ________mg of cholesterol

a) 100 b) 200

c) 300 d) 350

244. The addition of sugar to an egg_____the heat stability of protein

a) Increase b) Decrease

c) Does not change d) Increase and then decrease

245. Refrigerated eggs may retain quality as long as

a) 2 months b) 4 months

c) 6 months d) 8 months

246. Addition of acid to egg white is increased, the volume is

a) Stable b) Unstable

c) No change d) None of the above

247. Addition of fat interferes with______ foam formation

a) Increased b) Decreased

c) Does not change d) Increase and then decreased

248. The major protein actin constitutes ___________of myofibrils

a) 10% b) 15-20%

c) 30% d) 45%

249. The constituent of ligament is

a) Collagen b) Elastin

c) Albumin d) Globulin

250. Which of the following carbohydrate is present in meat

a) Glucose and glucose b) Glycogen and glucose

c) Glucose and galactose d) Glucose and mucin

Answers

1. d 2. a 3. b 4. a 5. b 6. a 7. d 8. c 9. c 10. a

11. c 12. d 13. b 14. b 15. c 16. a 17. d 18. c 19. c 20. c

21. c 22. d 23. c 24. a 25. c 26. c 27. a 28. a 29. b 30. b

31. c 32. d 33. b 34. b 35. c 36. c 37. b 38. a 39. c 40. d

41. d 42. c 43. a 44. c 45. b 46. c 47. b 48. d 49. c 50. b

51. a	52. a	53. b	54. c	55. c	56. c	57. a	58. a	59. d	60. a
61. c	62. d	63. d	64. a	65. b	66. b	67. b	68. a	69. d	70. b
71. d	72. b	73. c	74. d	75. d	76. a	77. c	78. c	79. a	80. b
81. a	82. a	83. a	84. b	85. a	86. c	87. a	88. a	89. a	90. d
91. d	92. d	93. b	94. c	95. a	96. d	97. d	98. a	99. b	100. b
101. b	102. a	103. d	104. d	105. d	106. b	107. a	108. a	109. b	110. b
111. a	112. b	113. b	114. d	115. c	116. b	117. b	118. d	119. b	120. c
121. b	122. b	123. a	124. a	125. c	126. d	127. a	128. a	129. a	130. a
131. b	132. c	133. c	134. b	135. d	136. d	137. b	138. a	139. a	140. c
141. b	142. a	143. c	144. a	145. c	146. d	147. a	148. d	149. b	150. d
151. a	152. b	153. c	154. b	155. a	156. c	157. d	158. d	159. a	160. a
161. b	162. b	163. b	164. d	165. d	166. c	167. d	168. b	169. c	170. d
171. b	172. b	173. a	174. b	175. d	176. a	177. d	178. c	179. b	180. b
181. a	182. c	183. d	184. c	185. d	186. b	187. d	188. a	189. a	190. a
191. d	192. c	193. a	194. c	195. c	196. d	197. a	198. a	199. b	200. b
201. d	202. d	03. c	204. b	205. a	206. a	207. b	208. d	209. b	210. b
211. b	212. c	213. c	214. d	215. a	216. b	217. b	218. d	219. b	220. a
221. a	222. d	223. d	224. a	225. a	226. b	227. c	228. b	229. b	230. b
231. d	232. d	233. d	234. a	235. c	236. b	237. d	238. a	239. c	240. c
241. a	242. b	243. a	244. a	245. c	246. a	247. b	248. b	249. b	250. b

2

Nutrition Science

1. Father of green revolution is ________.
   a) V.N. Patwardhan b) C. Gopalan
   c) S.G. Srikantia d) M.S. Swaminathan
2. ______ can affect both the nonspecific as well as the antigen specific components of the immune system.
   a) Overnutrition b) Undernutrition
   c) Malnutrition d) Minerals
3. National nutrition week is celebrated on _______.
   a) 1 to7th January b) 1 to 7th December
   c) 1 to 7th March d) 1 to 7th September
4. _______ state is a continuous phase in smoke.
   a) Liquid b) Semi-soild
   c) Soild d) Gas
5. RDA is revised by an expert group of _______.
   a) NIN b) ICMR
   c) WHO d) ICDS
6. Inhibitory factors like_______ is present in plant food which interferes with absorption of nutrients.
   a) Tannins b) Phytates
   c) Antitrypsin d) All of above
7. _____ act as precursor interrelationship nutrients.
   a) Vitamin C & iron b) Folic acid and iron
   c) Tryptophan & niacin d) Zinc & copper
8. There are over __________essential nutrients supplied by food.
   a) 20 b) 30
   c) 40 d) 60

9. The energy content of a food is measured in terms of its

a) Diet balance b) Fat

c) Fuel value d) None

10. The basal metabolic rate is ________in adults

a) High b) Low

c) Constant d) None

11. The science of nutrition deals with

a) Nutrition we need b) How much need

c) Where we get them d) Ali the above

12. Minerals are ____________nutrients

a) Inorganic b) Organic

c) Chemicals d) None of the above

13. For every 10^{0}c fall in environmental temperature, calorie intake is increased by

a) 1% b) 3%

c) 5% d) 7%

14. Vitamins are ____________nutrients

a) Inorganic b) Organic

c) Chemicals d) None of the above

15. A cheap substitute of butter is

a) Ghee b) Khoa

c) Vegetable oil d) Margarine

16. An unsaturated fat becomes saturated if it combines with

a) Hydrogen b) Nitrogen

c) Oxygen d) Carbon

17. Which of the following is not a source of carbohydrate?

a) Jaggery b) Potato

c) Starch. d) Fibre

18. Who determined the respiratory quotient?

a) Lavoisier b) Liebig

c) Regnault d) Carl Voit

19. Energy intake must be adequate for proper utilization of_____.
   a) Vitamin b) Protein
   c) Minerals d) Fat

20. Reference man is between _____ years of age.
   a) 20-25 b) 20-39
   c) 25-30 d) 20-35

21. Empirical formula for glucose______.
   a) $C_6 H_{12}O_6$ b) $C_{11}H_{22}O_{12}$
   c) $C_{12}H_{22}O_{11}$ d) $C_5H_{12}O_7$

22. ______ is known as mushroom sugar.
   a) Lactose b) Maltose
   c) Trehalose d) Sucrose

23. Glucose is also known as _____.
   a) Dextrose b) Fructose
   c) Galactose d) Mannose

24. Each gram of carbohydrate sugar or starch oxidized yields_____ calories.
   a) 4 kilo calories b) 9 Kilo calories
   c) 4.5 Kilo calories d) 5.5 Kilo calories

25. Main source of energy for central nervous system is ______.
   a) Fat b) Glucose
   c) Vitamins d) Carbohydrate

26. ____ can lead to irreversible damage to the brain tissue.
   a) Hyperglycemia b) Hypoglycemia
   c) Ketosis d) Ketonic acid

27. ____ is the major source of energy for muscle work.
   a) Fat b) Carbohydrate
   c) Minerals d) Vitamin

28. During muscular contraction glycogen is broken down to ______acid.
   a) Butyric acid b) Lactic acid
   c) Acetic acid d) Butaric acid

29. In adult man calcium turnover is normally from ______ mg daily.
    a) 400-500 b) 300-400
    c) 400-600 d) 500-600
30. Thrombin is an enzyme that converts a soluble blood protein called______.
    a) Fibrin b) Fibrinogen
    c) Thromboplastin d) Thrombosis
31. ______ is involved in the absorption of vitamin B12.
    a) Potassium b) Iron
    c) Magnesium d) Calcium
32. Physiological changes due to calcium balance occur in______.
    a) Growth b) Pregnancy
    c) Lactation d) All
33. About ______ gram of glycogen is stored in muscle.
    a) 150 b) 160
    c) 140 d) 130
34. Glycogen is stored in human liver is about ______ gram.
    a) 80 b) 60
    c) 90 d) 65
35. Fasting blood glucose level is between______.
    a) 80 – 100 mg/dl b) 80-120 mg/dl
    c) 90-140 mg/dl d) 90-120 mg/dl
36. Gluconeogenesis occurs in ______.
    a) Liver b) Kidney
    c) Small intestine d) Both a & b
37. Synthesis of fat from glucose is______.
    a) Lipogenesis b) Lipolysis
    c) Glucogenesis d) Gluconeogenesis
38. Level of ketone bodies in the blood of a normal person is about ______ mg/100ml.
    a) 2 b) 3
    c) 4 d) 5

39. Unsaturated fats are liquid at______.

a) Above 120º b) Boiling point

c) Room temperature d) 50°C

40. Fats from fish have a high proportion of PUFA containing _____ carbon atom.

a) 20-24 b) 15-25

c) 25-30 d) 30-35

41. TPN means _____.

a) Tender Proper Nutrition b) Tender Parenteral Nutrition

c) Total Proper Nutrition d) Total Parenteral Nutrition

42. ______ mg of calcium is prescribed for postmenopausal women.

a) 1000-1500 b) 500-800

c) 800-900 d) 500-1000

43. Each gram of haemoglobin contains about____ mg of iron.

a) 2.24 b) 3.4

c) 4.45 d) 3.33

44. Plant produces carbohydrate through the process called______.

a) Photosynthesis b) Phytosynthesis

c) Both a & b d) None

45. ____ sugar are widely distributed in nature.

a) Grape sugar b) Corn sugar

c) Both d) None

46. Starch is hydrolysed by ____ enzyme present in saliva.

a) Lactase b) Maltase

c) Amylase d Sucrase

47. ______ is the most important source of carbohydrate.

a) Pulses b) Cereals

c) Legumes d) Roots and tubers

48. _____gram of carbohydrate is needed in the diet to ensure the efficient oxidation of fats.

a) 50 b) 100

c) 150 d) 200

49. Liver is more resistant to certain poisons such as _______.
    a) Carbon
    b) Tetrachloride
    c) Alcohol
    d) All
50. _______ enzyme is present in the saliva.
    a) Ptyalin
    b) Amylase
    c) Maltase
    d) Sucrase
51. The absorption of glucose is affected by the amount of _____ions in the intestinal lumen.
    a) Sodium
    b) Potassium
    c) Both a & b
    d) None of these
52. About ______ % of CHO is digested and absorbed.
    a) 80-85
    b) 97-98
    c) 80-90
    d) 50-55
53. The complete oxidation of one molecule of glucose produces ______ATP molecules.
    a) 26
    b) 27
    c) 36
    d) 30
54. The precursor of niacin is
    a) Pyridoxine
    b) Riboflavin
    c) Tryptophan
    d) Leucine
55. Pantothenic acid is found in
    a) Liver
    b) Kidney
    c) Spleen
    d) All the above
56. Which of the following is called as vitamin H
    a) Choline
    b) Panthothenic acid
    c) Biotin
    d) Inositol
57. Oils are liquid at ______ degree.
    a) 10
    b) 20
    c) 25
    d) 30
58. On a mixed diet the calorigenic effect of food is about _____ percent.
    a) 15
    b) 10
    c) 20
    d) 25

59. Protein in food increase the metabolic rate is about ______ %.

a) 30 b) 20

c) 15 d) 10

60. ______ helps to enhance the absorption of calcium.

a) Lactose b) Maltose

c) Fructose d) Sucrose

61. Which of the following is characteristic of fats?

a) Hardness b) Hydrogenation

c) Emulsification d) All of these

62. Healthy non obese men have about ____ % of the body weight due to fat storage.

a) 15-20 b) 20-25

c) 10-15 d) 15-25

63. The layer of fat is very effective in ____.

a) Conductor b) Insulator

c) Both a & b d) None of these

64. Application of heat to protein causes_____.

a) Coagulation b) Shrinkage

c) Both and b d) None

65. _____ will eventually reduce the nutritive value of protein.

a) Boiling b) Steaming

c) Germination d) Roasting

66. _____ inhibitors are destroyed by heat during cooking.

a) Trypsin b) Chymotrypsin

c) Saponins d) None

67. Protein splitting enzymes is absent in ______.

a) Small intestine b) Large intestine

c) Saliva d) Stomach

68. The life span of RBC is about_______.

a) 100 days b) 120 days

c) 130 days d) 140 days

69. Oxalic acid is an organic acid found in _____.

a) Spinach b) Rhubarh

c) Chocolate d) All

70. Goitre control programme was introduced in India in the year _____.

a) 1962 b) 1972

c) 1979 d) 1980

71. The speed of the involuntary activity is controlled by hormone _____.

a) Thyroxin b) Oxytocin

c) ATH d) Cortisol

72. _____ is the device used to measure the heat of combustion.

a) Direct calorimeter b) Indirect calorimeter

c) Bomb calorimeter d) Calorimetery

73. Which of the following are organic nutrients?

a) Vitamins b) Minerals

c) Both a & b d) Hormones

74. According to ICMR _____ grams of protein per kilogram is needed for healthy adult.

a) 1.0 b) 2.0

c) 3.0 d) 4.5

75. Protein consists of _____ % of nitrogen.

a) 15 b) 16

c) 20 d) 25

76. _____ cannot be stored in the body.

a) Protein b) Fat

c) Carbohydrate d) None

77. There are _____ essential amino acids.

a) 10 b) 20

c) 15 d) 25

78. _____ is the simple protein.

a) Albumin b) Globulin

c) Glutelins d) All

79. Kilocalories can be defined as the amount of heat required to raise the temperature of _______kg of water by 1 degree Celsius.

a) 2 b) 1

c) 3 d) 2.5

80. The physiological fuel factors is derived and first felt by person at water is called_______ factors.

a) Direct calorimeter b) Indirect calorimeter

c) Atwater d) None

81. BMR is measured by an instrument called as______.

a) Direct calorimeter b) Indirect calorimeter

c) Benedict Roth Spriometer d) Bomb calorimeter

82. In last trimester of pregnancy BMR increased by ____ %.

a) 15-10 b) 115-25

c) 20-25 d) 10-15

83. BMR speeded up by ______% during hyperthyroidism.

a) 75-90 b) 70-75

c) 20-25 d) 10-15

84. When any food is ingested it result in the increase of heat production is called as________.

a) Calorigenic b) SDA

c) Thermogensis d) All of these

85. _____ acid has essential fatty acid properties.

a) Linolenic b) Linoleic

c) Fatty acid d) Omega 3 fatty acid

86. Fatty fish are good source of_____.

a) Omega 3 fatty acid b) Cholesterol

c) Triglyceride d) PUFA

87. _____ act as the role in regulating cell permeability.

a) Phospho lipids b) Omega 3 fatty acid

c) Cholesterol d) Carbohydrates

88. Lipoproteins are synthesized in _____.

a) Liver b) Large intestine

c) Small intestine d) Lung

89. Protein is composed of ______ compounds.

a) Carbon
b) Oxygen
c) Nitrogen
d) All of these

90. ____ simple protein is present in connective tissues.

a) Keratin
b) Elastin
c) Zein
d) Glaidin

91. Which of the following considered as complete protein?

a) Meat
b) Egg
c) Milk
d) All of these

92. Complete protein is also called as ______ foods.

a) High BV
b) Low BV
c) Medium BV
d) Very low BV

93. _____ maintains body resistance to disease.

a) Immunoprotein
b) Contractile protein
c) Normal protein
d) All of these

94. Nuts and oil seeds contain ______ % of protein.

a) 18-40
b) 15-30
c) 16-35
d) 20-30

95. ____ helps to calculation of net available protein of the diet.

a) Biological Value
b) Net Protein Utilization
c) Protein Efficiency Ratio
d) Net Protein Ratio

96. Ten gram of iodized salt provide ____ gram of iodine.

a) 100
b) 150
c) 110
d) 140

97. Infectious hepatitis is caused due to _____.

a) Mycotoxin
b) Utensils
c) Micro organism
d) Viral infection

98. Antioxidant is ______.

a) Vitamin K
b) Vitamin E
c) Vitamin B_1
d) Vitamin H

99. Purpose of diet therapy is to ______.
    a) Maintain nutritional status
    b) To correct the deficiencies
    c) To provide rest to whole body
    d) All of these

100. ________is an impairment of health resulting from a deficiency, excess or imbalance of nutrients.
    a) Malnutrition b) Over nutrition
    c) Both a & b d) All of these

101. The contraction of muscular walls of the digestive organs is stimulated by
    a) Celluloses b) Hemicelluloses
    c) Fibre d) All the above

102. Basal metabolism is calculated when
    a) Person is mentally and physically at rest
    b) Mental activity active
    c) Person is physically active
    d) None of the above

103. Which among them is a polysaccharides
    a) Cellulose, hemicellulose b) Fructosans, galactans
    c) Pentosans ,pectins d) All the above

104. Which among the following is called animal starch
    a) Dextrins b) Glycogen
    c) Caramel d) Cellulose

105. Deficiency of essential fatty acids leads to a skin condition known as
    a) Ketosis b) Phrynoderma
    c) Rancity d) Osteoporosis

106 Saturated fatty acids
    a) Elevate blood cholesterol
    b) Minimize the level of blood cholesterol
    c) Has no effect
    d) None of the above

107. Which of the following contain high proportion of polyunsaturated fatty acids

a) Groundnut oil b) Sesame oil

c) Safflower oil d) All the above

108. Which are the disease caused by fat deficiency

a) Eczema b) Phrynoderma

c) Dryness of skin d) All the above

109. What is $C_{27}H_{45}OH$

a) Oleic acid b) Stearic acid

c) Cholesterol d) Butyric acid

110. Adipose tissue which are mainly triglycerides are stored

a) Under the skin b) Around the organs

c) In abdominal cavity d) All the above

111. Nutritive value of the protein in legumes will be improved by

a) Diet planning b) Eating raw

c) Heat processing d) Soaking

112. Keratomalacia is caused due to

a) Deficiency of Vitamin A b) Deficiency of Vitamin D

c) Deficiency of Vitamin C d) Deficiency of Vitamin E

113. Some of the oxalate rich foods is

a) Gingelly b) Spinach

c) Amaranth d) All the above

114. A pregnant woman should avoid

a) Spicy food b) Deep fried food and sweets

c) Stale food d) All the above

115. Insufficient food intake could be due to

a) Missed meals b) Poor health practice

c) Poor schedule d) All the above

116. When there is insufficient energy supply the adults show

a) Reduced activity b) Slow deliberate movement

c) Avoidance of continuous effort d) All the above

117. Strontium 90 is a

a) Vitamin b) Radioactive fallout
c) Medicine d) Mineral

118. ____ helps in the lubrication of gastrointestinal tract.

a) Vitamins b) Minerals
c) Fat d) Carbohydrate

119. During the absorption process ______ are re-synthesized into triglycerides.

a) Fatty acid b) Glycerol
c) Monoglyceride d) All

120. The digested products are absorbed through the walls of _______.

a) Large intestine b) Small intestine
c) Lymph d) Liver

121. Hepatitis A is due to _____.

a) Parental route b) Contamination of food and water
c) Micro organism d) Oral route

122. Meal planner should have knowledge of pleasing combination in term of ____.

a) Texture b) Flavour
c) Method of preparation d) All of these

123. ____ stays in stomach for longest time.

a) Carbohydrate b) Protein
c) Fat d) Vitamins

124. Availability of food depends on _____.

a) Season b) Temperature of place
c) Location d) All of these

125. ____ is involved with carbohydrate metabolism.

a) Thiamin b) Iron
c) Niacin d) Cobalt

126. Growth of any organs or tissue where there is increase in cell number is known as_____.

a) Hypertrophy b) Hyperplasia
c) Hypo placid d) Hypotrophy

127. Nicotine and carbon-monoxide together produce____.

a) Hypoxia b) Hyperoxia

c) Both a & b d) None of these

128. Caffeine is present in_______.

a) Coffee b) Tea

c) Coca cola d) Milk

129. ______ responsible for biological reaction in body.

a) Riboflavin b) Vitamin K

c) Vitamin C d) All of these

130. 60mg of tryptophan is equal to ____ mg of niacin.

a) 1 b) 2

c) 4 d) 1.5

131. Vitamin B6 act as coenzyme for several reactions concerned with _____ metabolism.

a) Amino acid b) Fat

c) Protein d) Minerals

132. ______ increases the rate of neonatal death.

a) Premature labor b) Prolonged labor

c) Both a & b d) None of these

133. 2 g of haemoglobin provides ______mg of iron.

a) 3.4 mg b) 3 mg

c) 3.5 mg d) 4 mg

134. _____ is excreted through kidney.

a) Potassium b) Sodium

c) Magnesium d) Phosphorus

135. _____ is sunshine vitamin.

a) Vitamin A b) Vitamin B_2

c) Vitamin C d) Vitamin D

136. ____ vitamin is known as coagulation vitamin.

a) Vitamin A b) Vitamin D

c) vitamin K d) Vitamin E

137. Calcium absorption, depends upon ________.

a) Vitamin A b) Vitamin E

c) Vitamin D d) Vitamin K

138. Nursing mother secrete about ____ liter of milk per day.

a) 1/4 b) 1/2

c) 1/3 d) 1/5

139. Solid foods are normally introduced at _______ months.

a) 4-5 b) 5-6

c) 5-7 d) 4-6

140. Which of the following is liquid supplementary food?

a) Orange b) Cereals

c) Cucumber d) Carrot

141. Demineralization of bone is known as ______.

a) Osteoporosis b) Osteoarthritis

c) Osteomalacia d) None of these

142. Which of the following is acute fever?

a) Pneumonia b) Chickenpox

c) Typhoid d) All of these

143. An abnormal craving for substances which have little or no nutritional value is called______.

a) Pica b) Aeophagia

c) Both a & b d) None of these

144. Infant doubles the body weight in _______ months.

a) 5 b) 6

c) 4 d) 7

145. Heart beat of infant is about ________ beats.

a) 120-140 beats b) 130-140 beats

c) 120-125 beats d) 120-130 beats

146. Feeding behavior development depends on the_______.

a) Intestinal system b) Nervous system

c) Both a & b d) None of these

147. At birth baby can coordinated between _______.

a) Suckling b) Swallowing

c) Breathing d) All of these

148. Breast milk has lactoferrin which is an iron binding protein which hinders the growth of ______ in gut.

a) E.coli b) Bacteria

c) Both a & b d) None of these

149. Gerontology is science deals with _______ aspects of ageing.

a) Physiological b) Psychological

c) Sociological d) All of these

150. ______ is required for synthesis of nucleic acid.

a) Vitamin B_{12} b) Vitamin C

c) Folic acid d) Riboflavin

151. Fluoride is absorbed from the

a) Intestine b) Colon

c) Rectum d) Stomach

152. Fluoride is necessary

a) For healthy life b) For caries resistant teeth

c) To prevent edema d) All the above

153. People drinking soft water are prone to

a) Coronary heart disease b) Liver disease

c) Lung disease d) Skin disease

154. The vitamin responsible for anti sterility activity is

a) Vitamin A b.) Vitamin C

c) Vitamin D d) Vitamin E

155. Which of the following cannot be the cause of anemia

a) Hemorrhage b) Abnormal destruction of RBC

c) Iron deficiency d) Enlargement of the spleen

156. Heavy alcohol consuming people generally die of

a) Blood cancer b) Cirrhosis

c) Liver cancer d) Diabetes

157. Malabsorption of magnesium may occur in

a) Bowel resection b) Lactation

c) Malabsortion syndrome d) None of the above

158. One of the clinical manifestations of magnesium intoxication is

a) Lethargy b) Nausea

c) Vomiting d) Drowsiness

159. The serum level of manganese in 5ml is

a) 0.5 mcg b) 2.6 mcg

c) 0.5-2.6 mcg d) 2.6-3 mcg

160. The deficiency of manganese results in

a) Weakness of limbs b) Ataxia

c) Lack of balance d) All the above

161. Iron in food exists as

a) Organic porphyrin b) Inorganic salts

c) Hemoglobin d) Both a and b

162. Baby size who are less than _____ kg are called LBW.

a) 2.5 b) 2.6

c) 3.5 d) 3.6

163. ______ plays a role in reducing peroxidation reaction.

a) Vitamin E b) Selenium

c) Ascorbic acid d) All of these

164. Which of the following should be restricted during acute fever?

a) Fiber food b) Raw fruit and vegetables

c) Fried foods d) All of these

165. Food high in ______ should be avoided during cardiovascular disease.

a) Cholesterol b) Protein

c) Carbohydrate d) Minerals

166. IDDM occurs around the age of______.

a) 12 b) 30

c) 45 d) 50

167. Factors which will not affect BMR _______.

a) Sleep b) Age

c) Sex d) Hormones

168. Liver cancer is caused due to ______.

a) Meat b) Alcohol

c) Both a & b d) None of these

169. Among the followings who are the most prominent chances to brittleness of bones?

a) Children b) Adult

c) Elderly d) Women

170. Osteomalacia is caused by the deficiency of ________.

a) Vitamin A b) Vitamin K

c) Vitamin D d) Iron

171. Iron deficiency causes _______.

a) Anaemia b) Goitre

c) Cretinism d) Diabetes

172. Body temperature is regulated by_____.

a) Vitamin b) Fat

c) Water d) None of these

173. _________percent of additional calories are necessary for heavy physical activity.

a) 20-30% b) 25-50%

c) 30-35% d) 40-50%

174. Diarrhoea is caused due to _______.

a) Bacterial infection b) Protozoal infection

c) Parasitic infection d) All of these

175. Which of the following comes under liver function?

a) Detoxification b) Immunological function

c) Minerals & vitamin metabolism d) All of these

176. During jaundice plasma rises about _______ mg.

a) 20 b) 30

c) 35 d) 40

177. ______ caused due to the blockage of the bile flow between the liver and duodenum.

a) Hemolytic jaundice b) Obstructive jaundice

c) Hepatocellular jaundice d) All the above

178. Liver disorder leads to ______.

a) Lassitude b) Weakness

c) Fatigue d) All of these

179. Atherosclerosis is a pathological process in ______.

a) Coronary arteries b) Cerebral arteries

c) Aorta d) All of these

180. ____ required for replacement of amino acids and fat.

a) Pyloric obstruction b) Intestinal fistula

c) Both a & b d) None of these

181. ____ hydrolysis helps in the healing of abnormal wounds.

a) Protein b) Glucose

c) Both a & b d) None of these

182. ____ indicates the disease of colon.

a) Diarrhoea b) Dysentery

c) Constipation d) None of these

183. _____ occur in individuals fast for long period of time.

a) Duodenum ulcer b) Peptic ulcer

c) Both a & b d) None of these

184. Vitamin B_{12} is reduced in _____ condition.

a) Jaundice b) Cirrhosis

c) Obesity d) Underweight

185. Excess deposition of _____ result in Von Gierke's disease.

a) Glucose b) Glycogen

c) Fat d) Vitamin

186. ________ are characterized as a syndrome of disorder consciousness.

a) Hepatic precoma b) Coma

c) Both a & b d) None of these

187. In the condition of hepatic coma ______ is increased in patients.

a) Urea b) Ammonia

c) Sulphates d) Magnesium

188. In____ condition renal failure is common after surgery.

a) Hepatic coma b) Heptocellular jaundice

c) Obstructive jaundice d) Haemolytic jaundice

189. Phosphorous helps in ________.

a) Blood coagulation b) Tissue metabolism

c) Fluid balance d) Electrolyte balance

190. National AIDS control programme was launched in _________.

a) 1986 b) 1987

c) 1988 d) 1990

191. The Prophylaxis programme was launched during ___ five year plans against anaemia.

a) 1st b) 2nd

c) 3rd d) 4th

192. Ascariasis is an infection of the ______.

a) Intestinal tract b) Respiratory tract

c) Eye d) Lung

193. Tuberculosis can be identified by ______.

a) Matoux test b) Schick test

c) Both a & b d) ELISA

194. When did the WHO declared global eradication of small pox?

a) 5th May,1979 b) 6th May,1980

c) 18th june,1981 d) 8th May 1980

195. PEM is classified based on ______.

a) Gomez's classification b) Waterlows classification

c) McLarens classification d) All the above

196. The quantity of excreted water through perspiration is ______.

a) 200-300 ml b) 300-400 ml

c) 400-700 ml d) 700-900 ml

197. Calcium is necessary for _______.

a) Fluid balance
b) Haemoglobin formation
c) Growth in children
d) Acid base balance

198. ______ colour in fruits is due to the presence of flavanoids.

a) White
b) Red
c) Blue
d) Yellow

199. Biotin deficiency leads to _____.

a) Dementia
b) Dermatitis
c) Fatty liver
d) Cirrhosis of the liver

200. _______ is a formyl derivative of tetrahydrofolic acid.

a) Folic acid
b) Folinic acid
c) Pteroylglutamic acid
d) Glutamic acid

201. _______ leads to the condition of softening of cornea.

a) Bitots spot
b) Night blindness
c) Keratomalacia
d) Xeropthalmia

202. Riboflavin is not found in _______.

a) Fish
b) Apple
c) Milk powder
d) Yeast

203. ______ mg of iron is lost during parturition.

a) 200
b) 300
c) 400
d) 500

204. Thyroid gland can be prevented from intake of iodine by_____.

a) Radio-iodine
b) Perchlorate
c) Thiourea
d) None of these

205. The serum level of manganese in 5 ml is about ______.

a) 0.5 mcg
b) 2.6 mcg
c) 0.2-4.5 mcg
d) 0.5-2.6 mcg

206. Magnesium salts should be avoided in the condition of ______.

a) Oliguria
b) Anuria
c) Cyanosis
d) All of these

207. The intake of water level varies according to ______.

a) Dietary habits b) Climate

c) Body build and activities d) All the above

208. ______ is not a primary function of protein.

a) Repair of damaged parts

b) Replacement of worn-out and dead parts

c) Building of new materials for growth

d) To supply energy to the body

209. _____ is the commonest source of sodium.

a) Cheese b) Ham

c) Sea foods d) Salt

210. ________ condition leads to the cretinism.

a) Over activity of pancreas b) Over activity of thyroid gland

c) Over activity of adrenal gland d Under activity of thyroid

211. Which of the following factor helps to release energy from food?

a) Lymph b) Blood

c) Enzymes d) Hormones

212. In processing period which component of food stuff will be lost?

a) Vitamin b) Carbohydrate

c) Protein d) Fat

213. Which of following is not an international agency?

a) World bank b) UNICEF

c) WHO d) IAO

214. The National Filarial Control Programme (NFCP) was operated in the year____

a) 1945 b) 1955

c) 1975 d) 1976

215. Kala-azar is serious health problem in ____.

a) Maharashtra b) Biha

c) Orissa d) Karnataka

216. SNP for children was started in the year ______

a) 1950 b) 1955

c) 1960 d) 1970

217. To whom ICDS programme is beneficial?

a) Infant b) Adult

c) Adolescents d) Preschool children

218. CARE was established in ______.

a) 1940 b) 1942

c) 1946 d) 1948

219. Community development programme started in ______.

a) 1950 b) 1951

c) 1952 d) 1955

220. National Tuberculosis institute is located in ______.

a) Delhi b) Kerala

c) Bangalore d) Chennai

221. Name the place where training for filariology is given

a) Coimbatore b) Varanasi

c) Trivandrum d) Srinagar

222. The national malaria eradication programme was upgraded in

a) 1948 b) 1958

c) 1968 d) 1978

223. The acute respiratory disease control programme was started in the year

a) 1970 b) 1980

c) 1990 d) 2000

224. The STD control programme has been in operation in India since

a) 1940 b) 1949

c) 1954 d) 1959

225. Universal immunization programme was started in India in

a) 1965 b) 1975

c) 1985 d) 1995

226. The headquarters of ILO is in
a) Geneva b) New jersey
c) Rome d) Canada

227. The red cross home in South India is situated in
a) Chennai b) Bangalore
c) Hyderabad d) Trivandrum

228. This nutrient is needed for making hormones, healthier skin, and to make cell membranes:
a) Carbohydrate b) Fat
c) Vitamin B_{12} d) Fibre

229. The quality of protein assessed by
a) Amino acid score b) NPU
c) Both a and b d) None of the above

230. A growth chart has the potential use as
a) Growth monitoring b) Diagnostic test
c) Planning and policy making d) All the above

231. Haemoglobin is a ________ type of protein.
a) Animal protein b) Sinple protein
c) Derived protein d) Conjugated protein

232. Balwadi nutrition program is benefit for ____ age group of children.
a) 1-2 b) 2-3
c) 3-5 d) 3-6

233. In which year FAO was formed?
a) 1940 b) 1942
c) 1945 d) 1946

234. Which blood vessel in human body would normally carry the large amount of urea?
a) Hepatic vein b) Hepatic portal vein
c) Dorsal aorta d) Renal vein

235. In which year the Universal Child Immunization was started in India?
a) 1960 b) 1965
c) 1985 d) 1995

236. Chylomicrons are covered with a small layer of ________

a) Carbohydrate
b) Protin
c) Fat
d) Minerals

237. Which amino acid increases the metabolism of nicotinamide?

a) Lysine
b) Valine
c) Leucine
d) Serine

238. Softening of cornea leads to

a) Ketomalacia
b) Xeroderma
c) Dermatitis
d) None of the these

239. Hypernatremia results when the serum sodium rises

a) 150mEq/l
b) 160mEq/l
c) 165mEq/l
d) 170mEq/l

240. Estimation of magnesium can be carried out by

a) Colorimeter
b) Spectrometer
c) Spectrophotometer
d) Chromatography

241. NACO means

a) National Agenda Control Organisation
b) National Aids Conference
c) National Agenda Conference Organization
d) National Aids Control Organisation

242. Glycerol in food is detected by________.

a) Acolein Test
b) Zat's Test
c) Burchard Test
d) Salkowski Test

243. Pyenoid present in certain algae stores is

a) Starch
b) Vitamins
c) Minerals
d) Water

244. Salmonella are responsible for

a) Food allergy
b) Infection
c) Food poisoning
d) Diseases

245. 'Many vegetables can be dried by a process known as

a) Intrensive puffing
b) Explosive puffing
c) Hydro puffing
d) Puffing

246. Excessive administration of vitamin K results in
   a) Hyperthrombinemia b) Hypothrobinemia
   c) Kidneyfunction d) Diarrhea

247. Vitamin P is also called as
   a) Coagulant vitamin b) Permeability vitamin
   c) Solubility vitamin d) Sunshine vitamin

248. Excess of vitamin K does not raise the plasma____level
   a) Coagulants b) Anticoagulants
   c) Hormones d) Synthesis of prothrombin

249. Phosphorous aids in
   a) Tissue metabolism b) Blood coagulation
   c) Fluid balance d) Electrolyte balance

250. Urinary excretion of copper is increased by
   a Potassium sulphide b) Copper sulphide
   c) Penivillamine d) Thiocyanate

Answers

1. d	2. b	3. d	4. d	5. b	6. d	7. c	8. c	9. c	10. c
11. d	12. a	13. b	14. b	15. c	16. a	17. d	18. c	19. b	20. b
21. a	22. c	23. a	24. a	25. b	26. b	27. b	28. b	29. a	30. c
31. d	32. d	33. a	34. c	35. a	36. a	37. a	38. b	39. c	40. a
41. b	42. a	43. b	44. a	45. c	46. c	47. b	48. b	49. d	50. a
51. a	52. b	53. c	54. c	55. d	56. c	57. b	58. b	59. a	60. a
61. d	62. a	63. b	64. a	65. d	66. a	67. a	68. b	69. d	70. c
71. a	72. c	73. a	74. a	75. c	76. a	77. a	78. d	79. b	80. c
81. c	82. b	83. a	84. d	85. a	86. a	87. a	88. a	89. d	90. b
91. a	92. a	93. a	94. b	95. b	96. b	97. d	98. b	99. d	100. a
101. d	102. a	103. d	104. c	105. b	106. a	107. d	108. d	109. c	110. d
111. c	112. a	113. d	114. d	115. d	116. d	117. b	118. c	119. d	120. b
121. b	122. d	123. c	124. d	125. a	126. b	127. a	128. a	129. a	130. a
131. a	132. c	133. a	134. b	135. d	136. c	137. c	138. b	139. b	140. a
141. a	142. b	143. c	144. b	145. b	146. b	147. b	148. d	149. a	150. a

151. a	152. b	153. a	154. d	155. d	156. c	157. a	158. d	159. c	160. d
161. d	162. a	163. d	164. a	165. d	166. a	167. a	168. d	169. b	170. c
171. c	172. c	173. a	174. b	175. d	176. d	177. a	178. b	179. d	180. a
181. c	182. a	183. b	184. b	185. b	186. b	187. c	188. b	189. c	190. b
191. c	192. a	193. a	194. a	195. d	196. d	197. c	198. d	199. b	200. c
201. c	202. b	203. b	204. b	205. b	206. d	207. a	208. d	209. d	210. d
211. d	212. c	213. a	214. d	215. b	216. b	217. c	218. d	219. c	220. b
221. b	222. b	223. c	224. b	225. c	226. a	227. b	228. b	229. b	230. d
231. c	232. d	233. c	234. c	235. d	236. b	237. c	238. a	239. a	240. c
241. d	242. a	243. a	244. c	245. b	246. b	247. b	248. b	249. a	250. c

3

Textiles and Clothing

1. Fiber that are measured in miles or kilometers are

a) Stable Fibers b) Filament Fibers

c) Short Fiber d) Long Fiber

2. Denie is the term applied to the strength of

a) Fiber b) Yarn

c) Fabric d) Cotton

3. Caustic soda mercerization of cotton is carried out for improvement of a ______________

a) Strength and Luster b) Whiteness

c) Wetting d) None of the above

4 Texturizing is the processes that introduce

a) Coils b) Crimp

c) Zigzag shaping d) All the above

5. The primary property essential for a fiber is

a) Luster b) Density

c) Length to width ratio d) Resiliency

6. Cat tail is a _____fiber

a) Seed hair b) Bast

c) Leaf d) Animal hair

7. Any product capable of being spun, woven made into a fabric is ______.

a) Cotton b) Silk

c) Thread d) Fiber

8. Floats formed by weft yarns are ______.
   a) Satin b) Sateen
   c) Both a and b d) None
9. Spinning is the process it converts fibers into _______.
   a) Yarn b) Filament
   c) Thread d) None
10. Luster is the ________ textile fiber.
    a) Secondary b) Primary
    c) Miscellaneous d) None
11. The world's major textile fiber is _______.
    a) Cotton b) Wool
    c) Linen d) Spandex
12. Sunn is a______________
    a) Cellulosic fiber b) Protein fiber
    c) Mineral fiber d) Rubbet
13. Bending of yarn without breaking is ______.
    a) Cohesiveness b) Flexibility
    c) Both a & b d) None
14. Propane is the basis of _______ fiber.
    a) Poly propylene b) Poly ethane
    c) Poly methane d) Poly propylene
15. Wool can absorb up to ______% of its weight in moisture.
    a) 10 b) 20
    c) 30 d) 40
16. The high density fiber is
    a) Glass b) Cotton
    c) Acrylic d) Nylon
17. When the fiber molecules are arranged in random then it is
    a) High orientation b) Low orientation
    c) Crystalline d) Amorphous

18. Spot the odd one out
    a) Wet spinning b) Dry spinning
    c) Melt spinning d) Pad spinning
19. Cotton is affected by
    a) Alkalies b) Jute
    c) Strong acids d) All the above
20. China grass is
    a) Cotton b) Kapok
    c) Ramie d) Linen
21. Linen is the other name given to
    a) Cotton b) Flax
    c) Ramie d) Kapok
22. The short fibers are termed as
    a) Line b) Tow
    c) Filament d) Lint
23. In fabric form jute is frequently called
    a) Blended fabric b) Burlap
    c) Jute d) Kenaf
24. The fibre abaca is obtained from
    a) Sisal b) Banana
    c) Pineapple d) Jute
25. The fiber obtained from Angora goat is
    a) Alpaca b) Mohair
    c) Cashmere d) Angora
26. The resilience of wool is
    a) Good b) Moderate
    c) Fair d) Poor
27. The gummy substance which coats the silk fiber
    a) Pectin b) Glutin
    c) Serictin d) All the above

28. Degumming is carried out to remove

a) Pectin b) Glutin

c) Serictin d) None of the above

29. The resiliency of silk is

a) Very good b) Good

c) Moderate d) Poor

30. Silk is affected by

a) Alkalies b) Acids

c) Chlorine d) All the above

31. Ardil was made from the protein in

a) Casein b) Soya bean

c) Peanut d) Corn

32. Nomex is a

a) Nylon b) Ardil

c) Aramid d) Vinyon

33. Dacron and terylene belong to

a) Nylon b) Aramid

c) Vinyon d) Polyester

34. The natural mineral fiber is

a) Glass b) Asbestos

c) Carbon d) None of the above

35. Glass fiber is made from

a) Silica b) Limestone

c) Soda ash and borax d) All the above

36. The cloth straight from the loom is

a) Raw goods b) Finished fabric

c) Gray fabric d) None of the above

37. Thermoplastic property is exhibited by

a) Orlon b) Rayo

c) Cotton d) Silk

38. A process by which natural fibers are sorted and straightened is

a) Combing b) Grading

c) Ginning d) Carding

39. A best fiber obtained from agar plant is

a) Sisal b) Jute

c) Sunn d) Kapok

40. Spun yarns are composed of

a) Stable fiber b) Filament fibers

c) Low d) Thread

41. The only fiber which contains sulphur is

a) Cotton b) Jute

c) Silk d) Wool

42. Fibrolane is made using

a) Soya bean b) Groundnut

c) Casein d) Jute

43. Yarns composed of short, fibers are ________

a) Filament yarns b) Thrown yarns

c) Fancy d) Spun yarns

44. The desired diameter called the final draft is achieved during

a) Spinning b) Roving

c) Finisher drawing d) Carding

45. A slight amount of twist is imparted during ______________ operation

a) Finisher drawing b) Carding

c) Roving d) Drafting frame

46. Blending is carried out at __________ stage

a) Combing b) Carding

c) Finisher drawing d) None of the above

47. The most common adhesive used for twistles yarns is

a) Starch b) Olefin

c) Titanium dioxide d) None of the above

48. Two or more ply yarns twisted together gives________

a) Cord yarns b) Cable yarns

c) Both yarns d) None of the above

49. Crepe yarns are a variation of

a) Simple yarns b) Complex yarns

c) Ply yarns d) Cord yarns

50. Simple yarns is

a) Durable b) Produce smooth fabrics

c) Easy to care fabric d) All the above

51. Spinning quality is otherwise termed as ________.

a) Tenacity b) Adhesives

c) Cohesiveness d) None

52. Mass per unit volume is used to express ________.

a) Cohesiveness b) Density

c) Denacity d) All the above

53. ______ Fibers are measured either cm or inch.

a) Staple fiber b) Short fiber

c) Strong fiber d) Smooth fiber

54. What is Habutae?

a) Silk b) Cotton

c) Felt d) Polyester

55. The name for rayon in Europe is ________.

a) Spandex b) Viscose

c) Silk d) Polyester

56.______________ leads the world in man-made fiber production.

a) US b) China

c) Japan d) Taiwan

57. A type of warp knitting is ________.

a) Interlock b) Rib-knit

c) Tricot d) Float jacquard

58. Azlon refers to

a) Man made proteins fiber
b) Man made cellulosic fiber
c) Both a & b
d) None

59. This type of dyeing achieves a simple less expensive two colour pattern is ______.

a) Cross dyeing
b) Stock dyeing
c) Yarn dyeing
d) All

60. Polyester is resistant to ________

a) Weak alkalies
b) Weak acids
c) Strong acid at room temperature
d) All the above

61. Complex yarns primarily made for their ______?

a) Appealing
b) Appearance
c) Flexibility
d) Fashion

62. Cable yarns are otherwise called as ______.

a) Core yarns
b) Novelty yarns
c) Ply yarns
d) Cord yarns

63. Finisher drawing is done at the stage of _______.

a) Carding
b) Blending
c) Both a and b
d) None

64. Which of the following fibres has the smell of burning paper when it burns?

a) Nylon
b) Rayon
c) Acrylic
d) Cotton

65. Barium salts are ______.

a) Internal delustrant
b) External delustrant
c) Chemical modifier
d) All

66. Crinkled effect is produced by ______.

a) Basic finish
b) Alkaline finish
c) Acid finish
d) All

67. Decorating finish applied on ________.

a) Silk b) Rayon

c) Wool d) All

68. Lanolin is grease recovered and purified during the scouring process and used in ______.

a) Costume industry b) Cosmetic industry

c) Both a and b d) None

69. A minor amount of twist is imparted during ________.

a) Carding b) Drafting frame

c) Roving d) Finisher drawing

70. Flyer spinning is the oldest method which produced _______.

a) Smooth yarns b) Lustrous yarns

c) Both a & b d) None

71. The aristocrat of textile fabrics is ______.

a) Wool b) Silk

c) Laces d) Net

72. Complex yarns are otherwise called as _______.

a) Novelty yarns b) Core yarns

c) Ply yarn d) Cable yarns

73. Tensile strength is measured in ______.

a) Pounds per square inch b) Pounds per weight

c) Pounds per tex d) Pounds per inch

74. 50µm thickness filament gives a yarn structure like ______.

a) Too coarse b) Too thick

c) Coarse and thick d) None

75. Length to breadth ratio of cotton is ______.

a) 1500:2 b) 1500:3

c) 1500:1 d) None

76. Length to breadth ratio of wool is ______.

a) 3000:1 b) 3000:2

c) 3000:3 d) 3000:4

77. Length to breadth ratio of silk is ______.

a) $33 \times 10^3:1$ b) $33 \times 10^5:1$

c) $33 \times 10^6:1$ d) $33 \times 10^2:1$

78. Short lengthen fibers are called as ______.

a) Filaments b) Sample fibers

c) Both a & b d) None

79. Long lengthen fibers are called as ______.

a) Filaments b) Sample fibers

c) Both a & b d) None

80. Tenacity is measured by ______.

a) G/t b) G/w

c) W/g d) T/g

81. Strength of the fiber is also known as ______.

a) Tenacity b) Cohesiveness

c) Both a & b d) None

82. Strength of the fiber is directly related to ______.

a) Size of its polymers b) Length of its polymers

c) Both a & b d) None

83. Amorphous fibers are more ______.

a) Absorbent b) Weaker

c) Dyed d) All

84. Crystalline fibers are less ______.

a) Absorbent b) Stronger

c) Both a & b d) All

85. Example of stronger fiber when they are wet is ______.

a) Cotton b) Rayon

c) Wool d) Polyester

86. Example of weaker fiber when they are wet is ______.

a) Cotton b) Rayon

c) Wool d) Polyester

87. Secondary properties of fibers are ____.

a) Luster b) Density
c) Colour d) All

88. Spinning quality improvising fiber is also known as ______.

a) Magnet fibers b) Staple fibers
c) Filament d) None

89. Density is expressed by _____.

a) Gm/cm^3 b) Gm/cm^2
c) Gm/cm^5 d) Gm/cm^6

90. Brushing is a ________ finish

a) Chemical b) Mechanical
c) Non permanent d) None of the above

91. Mechanical finish is

a) Calendering b) Brushing
c) Catling d) All the above

92. Pressing is the term used for

a) Cotton b) Silk
c) Rayon d) All the above

93. Calendering is a __________ finish.

a) Durable b) Permanent
c) Renewable d) All the above

94. Carbonizing is a chemical finish applied to

a) Cotton b) Wool
c) Rayon d) All the above

95. Bleaching is done in ________ stage

a) Fiber b) Yarn
c) Fabric d) All the above

96. Hydrogen peroxide is a

a) Oxidative bleach b) Reductive bleach
c) Both a & b d) None of the above

97. Decating is the finish applied on

a) Wool b) Silk
c) Rayon d) All the above

98. The process involved in decating are

a) Heat and acid b) Pressure and heat
c) Pressure and moisture d) Pressure and acid

99. In scouring _______ is removed

a) Natural wax b) Dirt
c) Sizing d) All the above

100. In parching _______ imperfection is marked

a) Flaws b) Stains
c) Yarn knots d) All the above

101. The chemical finish which removes chemical from the fabric is

a) Bleaching b) Singering
c) Desizing d) Scouring

102. Silk is quite sensitive to heat due to the _______.

a) Lack of covalent cross-links b) Dryness
c) Crystalline polymer d) Resiliency

103. In silk the given symbol refers ⊠ _______.

a) Do not tumble dry b) Do not dry in direct sunlight
c) Both a & b d) None

104. Ⓟ, mean the silk _______

a) Should be dry cleaned b) Shouldn't dry cleaned
c) Should be pressed d) None

105. The symbol ⊠ indicates _______ the silk.

a) Do not dry cleaned b) Do not bleach
c) Do not use vinegar d) None

106. The sheared wool is called as _____.

a) Fleece b) Lecce
c) Fleche d) None

107. Wool is taken from slaughtered animal hide are called as ______.

a) Pulled wool b) Clipped wool

c) Class two wool d) Merino wool

108. Wool producing sheep may be classified into ______types according to the wool quality.

a) 4 b) 3

c) 5 d) 6

109. The first fleece sheared from a lamb about six to eight months old is known as_____wool.

a) Pulled b) Toglocks

c) Hogget d) Lamb's

110. A warp is made from______.

a) Pulled wool b) Lamb's wool

c) Dead wool d) Hogget wool

111. Weighting is a finish applied on

a) Cotton b) Silk

c) Wool d) All the above

112. Sizing involves the application of

a) Starch b) Resins

c) Dextrin d) All the above

113. Common method of polishing are__________

a) Cire b) Moire

c) Schreinering d) All the above

114. The cotton which undergoes basic finish is__________

a) Plissccreps b) Herberlin

c) Organdy d) All the above

115. An example of fabric treated with softener is __________

a) Plisse b) Orandy

c) Batiste d) All the above

116. The roots of fibers are generally damaged in ______.

a) Dead wool b) Pulled wool

c) Hogget wool d) Recycled wool

117. Irreversible shrinkage of the length, breadth and thickness of wool is called as______.

a) Felting of wool
b) Salting of wool
c) Fatling of wool
d) None

118. DFE stands for ______.

a) Directional Frictional Effects
b) Direct Frictional Effect
c) Direct Fitting Effect
d) None

119. [30] [40] [X], symbols in the wool_______.

a) Can be machine washed
b) Use wool detergents
c) Both a & b
d) The temperature must be below 30-40°C

120. Fibers shaven from living sheep can be labeled as _______.

a) Virgin wool
b) Blend wool
c) Coarse wool
d) Pulled wool

121. _______ is the first manmade fiber to be produced commercially.

a) Rayon
b) Acetate
c) Nylon
d) Polyester

122. The raw material can be made by mixing or dissolving natural fibers with some chemicals where they are called as _______

a) Regenerated fibers
b) Recycled fibers
c) Refined fibers
d) None

123. The moth proofing finish is done on

a) Rayon
b) Wool
c) Jute
d) All the above

124. Spinning is done by _____ different methods.

a) 3
b) 4
c) 5
d) 6

125. _______ was the first synthetic fiber.

a) Nylon
b) Polyester
c) Acetate
d) Rayon

126. Polyester is sometimes referred to as the_____fiber of the industry.
a) Work horse b) Big mixer
c) Mixed d) All

127. Yarns are divided into ______.
a) 2 b) 3
c) 4 d) 5

128. What are the two types of yarns ______?
a) Spun yarns and filamentous yarns
b) Monofilament and multifilament
c) Balanced yarns and un balanced yarns
d) None

129. Novelty yarns are usually ______ yarns, but they are not used to add strength to the fabric
a) Flock b) Spiral
c) Fly d) Slub

130. Which of the following fiber is most difficult to dye?
a) Cotton b) Nylon
c) Polyester d) None

131. Novelty yarns are also called as ______.
a) Fancy yarns b) Twisted yarns
c) Spiral yarns d) Flock yarns

132. Example of novelty yarns ______.
a) Chenille yarns b) Metallic yarns
c) Knop yarns d) All

133. ______________ are the steps involved in basic loom operation.
a) Shedding, picking and Battening
b) Spooling, Slashing and Warping
c) Warping, Slashing and Shedding
d) Slashing, Battening and Spooling

134. The actual repair of imperfections in the fabric is termed as
a) Buring b) Perching
c) Mending d) All the above

135. Functional finishes can be

a) Internal finish b) External finish

c) Chemical modifiers d) All the above

136. Example of basic weave is ______.

a) Plain weave b) Twill weave

c) Stain weave d) All

137. Basket and Rib weaves are two variations of ______.

a) Plain weave b) Twill weave

c) Stain weave d) None

138. Stain weave has ______ abrasion resistance.

a) Low b) Very low

c) Good d) Moderate

139. Plain weave has ______ abrasion resistance.

a) High b) Low

c) Moderate d) Nil

140. Cretonne, cheese cloth and Batiste are the examples of ______ weave.

a) Rib weave b) Plain weave

c) Basket weave d) Satin weave

141. What are the basic components require for knitting ______?

a) Yarn source and knitting elements

b) Fabric take

c) Fabric collection

d) All

142. ______types of needles that have evolved during the centuries.

a) 4 b) 3

c) 5 d) 6

143. Name the knitting needle used in the mechanical knitting loom____.

a) Bearded needle b) Latch Needle

c) Compound needle d) All

144. Which is the most successful needle among the following?

a) Bearded needle b) Latch Needle

c) Compound needle d) Latch and Bearded needle

145. The secondary property of a textile fiber is
a) Tenacity b) Luster
c) Propylene d) Uniformity
146. Tenacity is the term usually applied to the strength of
a) Fiber b) Yarn
c) Fabric d) Cotton
147. Texturizing is the processes that introduce
a) Coils b) Crimp
c) Zigzag shaping d) All the above
148. The common type of warp knitting is ________.
a) Double knit b) Tricot knit
c) Milanese knit d) None
149. Any product capable of being spun, woven made into a fabric is ______.
a) Cotton b) Silk
c) Thread d) Fibre
150. Floats formed by weft yarns are ______.
a) Satin b) Sateen
c) Both a and b d) None
151. Spinning is the process it converts fibers into ________?
a) Yarn b) Filament
c) Thread d) None
152. Dyes suitable for sublimation transfer printing are ____________
a) Acid dyes b) Disperse dyes
c) Direct dyes d) None of these
153. The processes of sanforization is used for ____________
a) Improvement in strength
b) Dimensional stability
c) Improvement in crease recovery
d) None of these
154. Decatising process is used for finishing of ______________
a) Cotton b) Wool
c) Polyester d) All of these

155. Limiting oxygen index is determined to test the efficiency of ______

a) Water and wear finishing b) Water proofing

c) Flame retardant finishing d) None of the above

156. Range of Maturity Ratio (M) of cotton is ______

a) 0 to 1 b) 0 to 100

c) 0.2 to 1.2 d) 0.5 to 1.5

157. Vat dyes are adapted to ______.

a) Cellulosic b) Acetate

c) Protein d) Polyester blends

158. Dispense dyes were originally developed for ______.

a) Silk b) Acetate fibers

c) Wool d) None

159. Dispense dye which is named as ______.

a) Acetate dye b) Acid dye

c) Basic dye d) Vat dye

160. Basic dyes are ______.

a) Acids b) Base

c) Salts d) All

161. Goddess of silk is ______.

a) Hungo-to b) Hu-ling-go

c) Si-ling-chi d) Fe-shi

162. Alum is a ______.

a) Mordent b) Dye

c) Pain d) All

163. Bacteriostat finish is carried out to ______.

a) Reduce infection b) Protect against mildew

c) Both a & b d) None of these

164. To obtain one gram of royal purple ______ animals are required

a) 12000 b) 13000

c) 14000 d) 15000

165. The first synthetic dye was synthesized by ______.

a) Sir Isaac Newton b) Sir William Perkin

c) Sir Isaac Perkin d) Sir William Henry

166. A substance which helps to fix the natural dyes to the fabric is ______.

a) Mordant b) Madder

c) Starch d) Gum

167. Mordant belong to the class ______.

a) Tannins b) Oils

c) Metallic salts d) All

168. Starched laundry can be dried in ______.

a) Tumble dryer b) Spray dryer

c) Vacuum dryer d) None

169. Durable fabrics are produced if starch is imparted in the ______.

a) Warp direction b) Weft direction

c) Both a & b d) None

170. A good standard elastic fabric should have a maximum growth of ______.

a) 12 % b) 8%

c) 4% d) 2%

171. A blue reactive dye indicated by CUP is ______.

a) Copper phthalocyanine b) Copper phosphate

c) Both a & b d) None

172. The resist printing technique which makes use of the wax is ______.

a) Screen printing b) Tie

c) Batik d) Dye

173. Removal of yarn knots are ______.

a) Burling b) Scouring

c) Decating d) Perching

174. The chemical which strengthens cotton is ______.

a) Alkali b) Acid

c) Soap d) None

175. The number of twist perinea for medium twist is ______ t.p.i.

a) 3-7 b) 3-12

c) 7-12 d) 0-3

176. The amount of twist depends on ________.

a) Type of yarn b) Size of the yarn
c) Mixing of yarns d) Inches of the yarn

177. If microscope test is not differentiating the fibers ________ is advisable

a) Solubility test b) Visual test
c) Burning test d) Yarn twist test

178. In which solvent viscose fiber is dissolved?

a) Concentrated nitric acid b) Cuprammonium
c) cuprammonium hydroxide d) Glacial acetic acid

179. The maximum 91% of cellulose is present in ________.

a) Wool b) Silk
c) Rayon d) Cotton

180. High density fabric gives ________.

a) Light a feel b) Heavies feel
c) Tight d) Coolest

181. Density is expressed as ________.

a) Selective mass per unit volume b) Mass per unit volume
c) None of above d) Both a and b

182. Convolutions meant ________.

a) Cotton ball opens b) Cylindrical ball shape
c) Yarn winding d) None of the above

183. The strength of the cotton can be increased by treating with caustic soda the process is called ________.

a) Convolution b) Mercerizing
c) Heat set d) Tendered

184. Sericulture is the term given to ________.

a) Cultivation of silk b) Processing of silk
c) Glows of silk warm d) Cocoon

185. Filature is the term, termed as ________.

a) Unwinding the filament b) Twisting the filament
c) Thickness of the filament d) None of the above

186. Removal of foreign matters is called ________.

a) Decating b) Scouring
c) Burling d) Perching

187. Silk fiber colour is turned into yellow is due to ______________.

a) Chlorine bleach b) Hydrogen peroxide
c) Per borate bleach d) All the above

188. The actual protein in silk is ________.

a) Tyrosine b) Alanine
c) Sericine d) Fibronini

189. Which tape is a stretchable knitted band?

a) Ripping tape b) Piping
c) Seam tape d) Measuring tape

190. Sericin is measured by ______.

a) Spinning b) Reeling
c) Degumming d) Throuing

191. Scouring is cleaning process of __________.

a) Silk b) Wool
c) Cotton d) Flax

192. The volatile solvents used for scouring are ________.

a) Benzene b) Petroleum naphtha
c) Carbon tetra chloride d) All the above

193. Wool is a protein called _______.

a) Keratin b) Alanine
c) Tyrosine d) Fibroin

194. Which tape is single or double folded?

a) Bias tape b) Twill tape
c) Piping d) None of these

195. Fibers are grouped and twisted together into a continuous stand called as ________.

a) Yarns b) fabric
c) Both a & b d) None

196. Example of textile materials which is made by yarns ________.

a) Knifed fabrics b) Monomers

c) Both a & b d) None

197. Fiber molecules are called ________.

a) Polymers b) Monomers

c) Both a & b d) None

198. Polymerization is the process of ________.

a) Joining of monomers end to end

b) Joining of mongers side by side

c) Joining of monomers end as well as side wise

d) All

199. Polymers are chemically ________.

a) Reactive b) Un reactive

c) Neither reactive nor unreactive d) None

200. DP stands for ______.

a) Degree of Polymerization b) Distance of Polymers

c) Depth of Polymers molecule d) None

201. Thermoplastic is made of ________.

a) Strong polymers b) Weak polymers

c) Crystalline d) All

202. Permanent creases and pleats can be made on fabrics containing ________.

a) Thermoplastic fibers b) Crystalline fiber

c) Both a & b d) None

203. After removal of heat the fiber hardens again and will remain the bent is called _____.

a) Heat set b) Hardening

c) Cooling d) None

204. Measurement of elongation is commonly made as ____________.

a) Elasticity to break b) Elongation to break

c) Stretching to break d) None

205. __________ indicates the percent of return from elongation to the original fiber length.

a) Elastic recovery b) Heat set

c) Thermal reaction d) Original length of fiber

206. Synthetic fibers can be divided up into______ fiber domains.

a) Two b) Three

c) One d) None

207. The most common method for introducing stretch in a fabric construction is ______.

a) Elastomeric rubber b) Heat setting

c) Knitting d) All

208. Removal of water mechanically is called_______.

a) Mangle b) Suction

c) Both a & b d) None

209. The size of the needle used for hand stitch is __________

a) No.4 b) No.8

c) No.7 d) No.5

210. What is the name for standard dart?

a) Full dart b) Half dart

c) French dart d) None of the above

211. Spinning of yarn means____________

a) Twisting b) Tex

c) Pulling d) None of these

212. The moth proofing finish is done on _______

a) Rayon b) Wool

c) Jute d) All the above

213. The leaf fiber is ____________

a) Jute b) Palm

c) Kapok d) All the above

214. __________ is the finish which does not allow water to pass

a) Stabilization finish b) Non shrinkage finish

c) Antistatic finish d) All the above

215. Which tape is used to reinforce the seam?
a) Piping b) Seam tape
c) Twill tape d) All the above

216. The impurity on wool termed suit is ___________
a) Dust b) Wool fat
c) Wool sweat d) All the above

217. The best soaps for degumming are those made from
a) Olive oil b) Tallow
c) Coconut oil d) None of the above

218. Soaps with strong alkali destroys the _____
a) Fibroin b) Casein
c) Pyrin d) Purine

219. Garment cutting and manufacturing is based on___________
a) Fit b) Measurements
c) Style d) All the above

220. Casual wear require at least ___________stretch
a) 10% b) 25%
c) 45% d) 55%

221. The first choice in fabric selection is
a) Colour b) Material
c) Weave d) Luster

222. Stretch is introduced in the yarn through
a) Use of electrometric rubber b) Heat setting
c) Knitting d) All the above

223. Stretch can be produced in
a) Warp direction b) Weft direction
c) Warp and weft direction d) All the above

224. Durable fabrics are produced if stretch is imparted
a) Warp direction b) Weft direction
c) Warp and weft direction d) All the above

225. Earlier dyes were obtained from __________

a) Animal sources b) Plant sources

c) Minerals d) All the above

226. Which of the following is animal give wool?

a) Sheep and yak b) Snake and duck

c) Cow and dog d) All of the above

227. The red dye obtained from the root of rubia

a) Madder b) Cochineal

c) Indigo d) Mordant

228. Adjective natural dye needs

a) Amordant b) No mordant

c) A acid d) An acid

229. Natural dyed fabric are

a) To stitch b) To bite

c) To dye d) All the above

230. Glauber salt is

a) Sodium chloride b) Sodium sulphate

c) Sodium hydroxide d) Sodium nitrate

231. A blank square over the warp is called as __________.

a) Sinker b) Raiser

c) Both a&b d) None

232. Weaves are basically divided into __________.

a) 3 b) 4

c) 2 d) 5

233. Which part of the jute plant does give fiber?

a) Root b) Leaf

c) Stem d) All the above

234. Nylon is a fabric whose filaments are prepared from __________.

a) Melt spinning b) Wet spinning

c) Blow spinning d) Spinning

235. "Chain Crass" is ________

a) Linen b) Kapok

c) Fiber d) Ramie

236. Polyester is referred as ________________

a) Acrylic b) Workhorse

c) DuPont d) None of these

237. When was first modern cotton textiles mill set up________

a) 1956 b) 1961

c) 1818 d) 1897

238. Which stitch is equivalent to machine stitch __________

a) Loop stitch b) Tailor taking

c) Back stitch d) All the above

239. Embroidering over gathers is called _____________

a) Smocking b) Lace

c) Appliqué d) None of these

240. Artificial silk is _____________

a) Acetate b) Polyester

c) Rayon d) Silk

241. The shape of the cotton under microscope is ______.

a) Kidney shape b) Irregular polygon

c) Rounded triangle d) Oval

242. The shape of the linen under microscope is ________.

a) Irregular polygon b) Rounded

c) Oval d) Fibrillar

243. The shape of the silk fiber under microscope is ________.

a) Bean b) Polygon

c) Triangle d) Rounded triangle

244. Silk has high luster, medium resiliency and elastic recovery of ______%.

a) 80 b) 70

c) 50 d) 90

245. Mohair is hairs of ______.

a) Hare b) Yak

c) Camel d) Goat

246. Nylon is a fabric whose filaments are prepared from ______.

a) Dry spinning b) Wet spinning

c) Blow spinning d) Melt spinning

247. A fabric used for outfit in Twill weave in wool or as a mixture is of light to medium weight and is raised from one or both sides is ______.

a) Afgalaine b) Tweed

c) Cheriot d) Flannel

248. Kapok is used chiefly in the manufacture of ______.

a) Mattresses b) Pillows

c) Both a and b d) None

249. Manila is ______.

a) Bast fiber from stems of a plant

b) Hair cells from a fruit plant

c) Hard fiber from coconut

d) All

250. Which embroidery is called white embroidery ______

a) Chikan work b) Kashida

c) Kasuti d) None of these

Answers

1. b	2. b	3. a	4. d	5. c	6. a	7. d	8. b	9. a	10. a
11. a	12. a	13. b	14. d	15. c	16. a	17. d	18. d	19. c	20. c
21. b	22. c	23. b	24. b	25. b	26. a	27. c	28. c	29. c	30. d
31. c	32. c	33. d	34. b	35. d	36. c	37. a	38. a	39. b	40. a
41. d	42. c	43. d	44. a	45. c	46. c	47. a	48. c	49. a	50. d
51. c	52. b	53. a	54. a	55. b	56. b	57. c	58. a	59. a	60. c
61. b	62. d	63. b	64. d	65. b	66. a	67. d	68. b	69. c	70. c
71. c	72. a	73. a	74. c	75. d	76. a	77. b	78. b	79. a	80. a
81. a	82. b	83. d	84. c	85. a	86. b	87. d	88. a	89. a	90. b

91. d 92. b 93. c 94. b 95. d 96. a 97. d 98. c 99. d 100. d
101. d 102. a 103. a 104. a 105. b 106. a 107. a 108. a 109. d 110. d
111. b 112. d 113. a 114. a 115. c 116. b 117. a 118. a 119. c 120. a
121. a 122. a 123. b 124. a 125. a 126. a 127. a 128. a 129. c 130. c
131. a 132. a 133. d 134. c 135. d 136. d 137. a 138. b 139. a 140. b
141. d 142. b 143. d 144. b 145. b 146. a 147. d 148. a 149. d 150. b
151. a 152. b 153. b 154. b 155. c 156. c 157. d 158. b 159. a 160. c
161. c 162. b 163. d 164. a 165. b 166. a 167. d 168. a 169. b 170. d
171. a 172. a 173. a 174. a 175. b 176. c 177. b 178. d 179. b 180. b
181. a 182. b 183. a 184. a 185. b 186. a 187. d 188. c 189. a 190. b
191. d 192. a 193. a 194. a 195. a 196. a 197. b 198. a 199. a 200. b
201. a 202. c 203. a 204. a 205. b 206. a 207. d 208. a 209. c 210. b
211. b 212. b 213. b 214. a 215. b 216. c 217. a 218. a 219. b 220. b
221. b 222. a 223. d 224. b 225. d 226. a 227. a 228. a 229. d 230. b
231. d 232. a 233. c 234. a 235. d 236. b 237. c 238. c 239. a 240. c
241. d 242. d 243. b 244. d 245. b 246. a 247. c 248. b 249. a 250. a

4

Family Resource Home Managemnt

1 Which of the following is associated with standard__________?

a) Tradition
b) Costume
c) Social
d) All of these

2. Which of the following is true about home management __________

a) Administrative
b) Mental work
c) Decision making
d) All of these

3. Who has written "what kind of Experience is economizing" __________

a) Nickel and Dorsey
b) L Macfie
c) Elizabeth E.Hoyt
d) Hiatt

4. While __________ home maker may see to it that plans are realistic and flexible

a) Planning
b) Control
c) Organizing
d) Evaluation

5. Social qualities imply that the home maker's __________

a) Vitality
b) Polite
c) Cooperative
d) None of these

6. __________ standards can be changed to suit different situation.

a) Freedom
b) Flexible
c) Choice
d) Both a and b

7. "According to __________ the hardest work of all is to think and decision making is thinking"

a) Hazel Kyrk
b) Iacque Barzun
c) George Soule
d) None of these

8. "Making management –Human" is a book by__________

a) Alfred J.Marrow
b) M Johnson
c) M.P.Follett
d) None of these

9. Who has written "The psychology of Thought and Judgement" ________

a) G.L.Johnson b) M. Johnson

c) H Knight d) None of these

10. Time is ________ unique resource, because it is equal to all.

a) Available b) Fixed

c) Unfixed d) Both a and b

11. Lifecycle categorized into ____________ in home management

a) 5 b) 6

c) 4 d) 3

12. A manual for training the disabled home maker was written by___ ___

a) N.C Landon b) Allan Mogenson

c) H.A Rusk d) None of these

13 Principles of Home management include________

i) Fulfilment of needs of the family members

ii) Keep a balance between family income and expenditure

iii) Top perform household work effectively

iv) Psychological satisfaction

a) i, ii ,iii, iv b) i, ii,iii

c) i, ii d) i, iv

14. The success of goal achievement depends upon __________

a) Cooperation b) Able leadership

c) Decision power d) All of the above

15. The important difference between a home and a house is ____________

a) Physical b) Environmental

c) Emotional d) Terminology

16. Who said with regard to spiritual values that the family is not only the best conveyer but is the producer of values______________

a) Lawrence Frank b) Leonard Mayo

c) Louis F.Roth d) William E.Engloreandso

17. Who stated this " life is characterised by the striving for goals"______

a) Lawrence Frank b) Dewitt H Parker

c) Nickell and Dorsey d) Goodyear and Kiohr

18. Home management is________

a) The administrative side of family living

b) It makes use of finding of science and knowledge of the different aspects of family of life

c) Planning controlling and evaluating the use of available to family for the purpose of attaining family goals.

d) All of above

19. Harmony is __________

a) Mood b) Spirit

c) Theme d) All of these

20. Money as a non human resource can be in the form of __________

a) Savings b) Wages

c) Income on investments d) All of these.

21. Community facilities as Non-human resource include__________

a) Libraries b) Parks

c) Shopping facilities d) All of these

22. Food, own house, car etc is example of__________

a) Non-human resource b) Material goods

c) Required different treatment d) All of these

23. A family that is willing to accept common and inexpensive foods get meals on a limited income. It is an example of __________

a) Attitude b) Poverty

c) Skill d) None

24. Which of the factor effect use of resource__________

a) Motivation

b) Capacity and philosophy

c) Life cycle and family factors like heritage

d) All of these

25. ______________ is essential for home management

a) Participation of the family members in decision making

b) Family working together for common purpose

c) Sharing of responsibilities

d) None of these

26. Which of the following is home maker functions__________

a) Producer b) Coordinator

c) Consumer d) All of these

27. Work Simplification can be grouped into 3 classes__________

a) Body position and motions sequence of work

b) Tools equipment and arrangement

c) Product

d) All of these

28. The term" peak load" refers to__________

a) Activity at home b) Activity at office

c) Activity at academic d) All of the above

29. It is a chart which shows step-by-step description of the method used in doing a task__________

a) Operation chart b) Process chart

c) Micro motion film d) None of these

30. It is used in making a more detailed study of some particular part of the process__________

a) Operation chart b) Process chart

c) Cyclograph d) None of these

31. According to WHO the energy expenditure for hard working women is__________

a) 225 b) 300

c) 325 d) 200

32. Operation chart helps in reduction of__________

a) Hard movement b) Eye movement

c) Body movement d) Work movement

33. ________________ is essential for saving time and energy

a) Controlling b) Planning

c) Organizing d) Delegating

34. Cyclograph records________________

a) Walking b) Running

c) Rhythmic stroke d) None of these

35. Who said "Decision is the smallest units of management" ________________

a) Esther Crew Brather b) Nickel

c) Mundal d) Dorsey

36. Decision making is greatly influenced by________

a) Goals b) Value

c) Standards d) All of these

37. Basically there are ____________ kinds of decision

a) 2 b) 3

c) 4 d) 5

38. The use of copper on these days ____________

a) Making utensils b) Making cutlery

c) Covering pans of other metals d) None of these

39. An efficient home maker is also a________________

a) Good decision maker b) Good director

c) Good conveyor d) All of these

40. Which one of the following is not a good method of money investment______________?

a) LIC b) FDR

c) NSC d) Lottery

41. The qualities of rust is/are________________

a) Reddish powder

b) Forms on iron

c) Formed when iron remains wet

d) All of these

42. Real income means flow of ________________

a) Satisfaction b) Money

c) Goods and service d) Goods

43. Income of a family is influenced by________________

a) Status of the family

b) Size of the family

c) Stage of the family

d) Locality in which the family lives

44. The material resource is otherwise called as________________

a) Human resource b) Non human resource

c) Both a and b d) None of these

45. In balance sheet annual statement of ________________are made at the end of the year

a) Assets b) Liabilities

c) Both a and b d) None of these

46. ________________ account is maintained on weekly or monthly basis

a) Ledger b) Balance sheet

c) Expenditure account d) Income

47. Which of the following comes under post office savings account ________________

a) Jeevanbava scheme b) Kisanvikaspatras

c) Indravikaspatras d) All of these

48. Forms are closely related with________________

a) Circles b) Square

c) Rectangle d) Lines

49. Line movement create________________

a) Rhythm b) Confusion

c) Both a and b d) None of these

50. Duplicate column and striped fabrics is an example of ________________

a) Proportion b) Balance

c) Rhythm d) None of these

51. Rhythm occurs in ______________

a) Regular repeated movement b) Variable transitional movement

c) Both a and b d) None of these

52. It is a sort of surface on enrichment ______________

a) Flower b) Lines

c) Pattern d) None of these

53. Fundamental or primary colours are ______________

a) Red b) Yellow

c) Blue d) All of these

54. Amount of lightness or darkness in colour is______________

a) Hue b) Complementary

c) Value d) None of these

55. The modern home has greatest ______________ implication

a) Physiological b) Psychological

c) Relaxation d) Both a and b

56. Home furnishing is a book by ______________

a) Anna Hong Rutt b) Ibid

c) Friedman d) None of these

57. "Home and character" is by______________

a) Friedman b) H.T Craug O.

c) Van Dommelen d) None of these

58. "Interior design" has been written by______________

a) Pramilamehra b) Friedman J.F Pile, F.Wilson

c) Rutt d) Ibid

59. The purpose of design is to make things beautiful is stated by ______________

a) Friedman b) Wilson

c) Pile d) All of the above

60. ______________ are the activities done in preparation area

a) Cutting b) Chopping

c) Serving d) Both a and b

61. Which is the example of intrinsic values?

a) Love b) Affection

c) Comfort d) All of these

62. Which of the following comes under moderate work?

a) Washing clothes b) Mopping

c) Grinding d) Ironing

63. Routine task at home is called as __________

a) Mental effort b) Manual effort

c) Tarsal effort d) Pedan effort

64. The pathway chart and cycle-graph are the techniques involved in __________ studies

a) Time and motion b) Motion and economy

c) Time and management d) None of these

65. In a pathway chart a thread is used to evaluate __________

a) Distance covered by the worker

b) Topic covered by the worker

c) Community covered by the worker

d) None of these

66. Which of the following lines suggest life and dignity __________

a) Diagonal b) Horizontal

c) Curved d) Straight Horizontal

67. __________ affects the use of money

a) Size and composition of a family

b) Status of a family

c) The availability of money and resource

d) All of these

68. Piggy bank deposit and fixed deposit account are example of __________

a) Post office saving account b) Provident fund account

c) Life insurance scheme d) Bank accounts

69. Money given to bank and deposit in your name is called__________

a) Cheque b) Pass book

c) Endorses d) Chit fund

70. Shares are __________ property

a) Stocks b) Binds

c) Transferable d) Untransferable

71. Basically there are __________ types of kitchen

a) 5 b) 6

c) 7 d) 10

72. The small house and apartments __________ types of kitchen preferred

a) One wall kitchen b) U shaped kitchen

c) L shaped kitchen d) Broken L shaped kitchen

73. __________ colours should be avoided from kitchen

a) Cool b) Warm

c) Absorbent d) Both a and b

74. The __________ lines gives rich effect

a) Diagonal b) Curved

c) Vertical d) All of these

75. While planning furnishing __________ is considered

a) Space b) Light

c) Pattern d) All of these

76. Texture generally leads one of thing to __________

a) Solid b) Tangible

c) Rigid d) Shine

77. Emphasis means__________

a) Centre point of attraction b) Happiness

c) Sorrowed d) Beauty

78. The necessity of curtains in the room is __________

a) Maintains the privacy b) Protects from dust

c) Enhance beauty d) All of these

79. Generally pattern should be used for about ______ of the total surface area

a) 1/2 b) 1/4

c) 1/3 d) 1/5

80. The harmony embraces ______________ aspects of design

a) 4 b) 5

c) 6 d) 10

81. The ratio considered most in interior decoration is ________

a) 1:5 and 1:3 b) 1:4 and 1:1

c) 1:2 and 1:1 d) 1:1 and 1:4

82. Which of the following statement is correct ______________

a) Smooth texture and dainty fabric blend wall

b) Hard texture and finds are harmonious

c) Form gives characteristic and beauty to object

d) None of these

83. Conventional standards are usually associated with______________

a) Tradition b) Custom

c) Social taboos d) All of these

84. A set of measures of values are called __________

a) Attitudes b) Standards

c) Morals d) None of these

85. In our daily life ____________ are motivating factors that influence our behaviour

a) Values b) Standards

c) Goals d) None of these

86. Owning a house is an example of______________

a) Short term goal b) Long term goal

c) Intermediate or end goal d) None of these

87. A __________ family is beneficial to child, family, society and nation

a) Small b) Big

c) Medium d) Nuclear

88. Knowledge, abilities and skills, energy and time are example of ________________.

a) Human resource b) Non-human resource

c) Both a and b d) None of these

89. In growing organisation, the specialized staff is needed by ________________

a) Line manager b) HR manager

c) Staff manager d) All of the above

90. A time plan usually involves________________

a) Types of activity and stages of life cycle

b) Peak loads

c) Leisure

d) All of the above

91. Bending, learning, sitting etc are examples of________________

a) Manual effort b) Tarsal effect

c) Real effort d) None of these

92. Time and energy can be saved by________________

a) Collecting everything you need before starting

b) Placing item at their point of use

c) Planning the sequence of your activities

d) All of these

93. Majority of the disputes in industries are related to the problem of ________________

a) Wages b) Salaries

c) Benefits d) All of these

94. Work simplification implies the use of ________________

a) Least time b) Least effort

c) Least energy d) All of these

95. The ________________ is the heart of the management

a) Organizing b) Selecting

c) Decision making d) Controlling

96. Factors affecting identification and understanding a problem is ______________

a) Home makers personality b) Individual differences

c) Age difference d) All of the above

97. Decision that are referred as habits that have become an established pattern of behaviour is __________

a) Conscious decision b) Routine decision

c) Immediate decision d) None of these

98. Record of all expenditure of a big nature is ____________

a) Income and expenditure account

b) A balance sheet

c) Ledger

d) None of these

99. A deposit for a predominant number of years and the payments to be made every month is_____________

a) Provident fund account b) Cumulative time deposit

c) Fixed deposit d) None of these

100. Special money boxes saving accounts, current accounts are example of_____________

a) Providing fund account b) Life insurance scheme

c) Post office saving account d) Bank accounts

101. High performance work system leads to______________

a) Superior employee performance

b) Low labor cost

c) Safe workplace

d) Less employee turnover rate

102. Techniques that helps to track down all wasteful expenditure of time and energy in all activities is__________________

a) Process chart b) Operation chart

c) Cyclograph d) Pathway chart

103. Factors affecting use of money is____________

a) The availability of money and resource

b) Size and composition of a family

c) Status of a family

d) All of these

104. Decision of family finances, problem of land and property division are example of__________.

a) Personal decision b) Collective decision

c) Routine decision d) None of these

105. Which of the statement is incorrect?

a) Among educated people the sharing for a decision is almost equal

b) Personal decision are more common in the later stages of family life cycle

c) Personal decision are simple and limited compared to those of collective decision

d) None of these

106. To keep records related to money a family may utilize __________

a) The income and expenditure account

b) A general ledger

c) A balance sheet

d) Any of these

107. A record of all expenditure of a big nature is__________

a) Income and expenditure account

b) A balance sheet

c) A ledger

d) None of these

108. Refraining from spending for consumption needs is called ________

a) Spend thriftiness b) Frugality

c) Saving d) Extravagance

109. Endowment policy, group insurance schemes, family pension scheme are example of _____

a) Units trust of India b) Life insurance scheme

c) Chit funds d) Provident fund account

110. A deposit for a pre dominant number of years and the payments to be made every month is__________

a) Provident fund account b) Cumulative time deposit

c) Fixed deposit d) Term deposit

111. Saving account IndriaVikaspatras cumulative time deposit is example of ________.

a) Provident fund account b) Post office saving account

c) Bank accounts d) Shares and debentures

112. The amount of land and space required for housing the family is affected by__________________

a) Size and composition of the family

b) Family's living habits

c) The activities to be carried on

d) All of these

113. The _________________ lines achieve a joyful , subtle and effect

a) Horizontal b) Curved

c) Diagonal d) Vertical

114. The __________________ is something solid and tangible

a) Texture b) Forrn

c) Pattern d) Space

115. Which statement is incorrect?

a) If walls are plain then draperies may be patterned

b) Forms are also called prints or designs

c) Naturalistic motifs look good in children's rooms

d) Stylized motifs are distorted

116. To be in harmony means__________________

a) To be in agreement b) To be pleasant

c) Both a and b d) None of the above

117. The" law of relationship" is also known as the principle of __________

a) Harmony b) Proportion

c) Balance d) Emphasis

118. The proportion is the ratio of ____________
   a) Comparative size
   b) One thing considered alongside another
   c) Both a and b
   d) None of the above

119. Space can be increased by ____________
   a) Using few partition
   b) Providing smaller openings between rooms
   c) Restricting glass walls
   d) None of these

120. Object which are not placed at equal distance, but placed in such that they appear in equilibrium is ____________
   a) Optical balance   b) Formal balance
   c) Informal balance   d) None of these

121. A balance arrangement provides a sense of ____________
   a) Arrogance   b) Restfulness and repose
   c) Instability   d) None of these

122. The ____________ is made up of size, form, colour and texture
   a) Structural design   b) Decorative design
   c) Both a and b   d) None of the above

123. Hue is also called as ____________
   a) Paint   b) Secondary colours
   c) Basic colours   d) Balance

124. When black is added to colour it produces ____________
   a) Tint   b) Shade
   c) Both a and b   d) None of these

125. The intensity of colour includes ____________
   a) Strength of a color   b) Purity of a color
   c) Both a and b   d) None of the above

126. The use of colour helps to achieve ____________
   a) Contrast   b) Blend
   c) Accent   d) All of these

127. The _________ colour gives coolness, limpness, dullness and feminity

a) Orange b) Red

c) Violet d) Brown

128. Which of the statement is incorrect?

a) Red colour has a stimulating or cheering effect

b) Green colour is symbolic of serenity and rebirth

c) Blue colour is an intellectual appeal

d) Yellow colour is depressing to morose

129. Equal balance of furniture gives a __________ to a room

a) Graceful effect b) Restful effect

c) Pleasing effect d) All of the above

130. Balance and stability of flower arrangement is __________

a) Virtual b) Actual

c) Lateral d) Both a and b

131. Line of furniture and decoration may be__________

a) Straight b) Curved

c) Parallel d) All of the above

132. The colour green represents__________

a) Serenity b) Depressive

c) Heroism d) Cheerfulness

133. The different style of flower arrangement is __________

a) Ikebana b) Moribana

c) Ohara d) All of the above

134. Floor decoration using rice powder is practised in__________

a) Kerala b) Karnataka

c) Tamil Nadu d) Orissa

135. Termites can be controlled by using__________

a) Sodium arsenate b) D D T

c) Pentachlorophen d) All of the above

136. Old furniture may be drenched in ______________ before refinishing

a) Petrol b) Coal tar

c) Kerosene d) Water

137. Tarnished fine brass can be cleaned with______________

a) Lemon juice b) Vinegar

c) Salt d) All of these

38. Copper vessels can be cleaned with__________

a) Salt b) Vinegar

c) Methylated spirit d) All of the above

139. The input of the family system are______________

a) Met demands b) Demands and resources

c) Used resources d) Personal system

140. The proportion of output re-entering the system as input to affect succeeding output is______________

a) Input b) Output

c) Feedback d) Resources

141. Planning is a series of decision concerning______________

a) Standards b) Sequence of action

c) Both a and b d) None of the above

142. The two components of implementing are______________

a) Evaluating b) Controlling

c) Facilitating d) Both b and c

143. Which of the following statement is correct regarding budget ______________?

a) Helps to live with in one's income

b) Helps to save

c) Gives the plan for spending and not for saving

d) Develops good buy man ship

144. Which of the following is not suitable for holding delicate flowers ______________

a) Pottery b) Bamboo containers

c) Glass containers d) Metal containers

145. Motivating factors of management are______________

a) Interest b) Attitude

c) Goals d) All of the above

146. Which one of the following is a chemical flooring__________?

a) Brick b) Marble

c) Mosaic d) Linoleum

147. A criteria closely related to structural design is____________

a) Beauty b) Durability

c) Functionalism d) Suitability

148. A tool of measuring work time is______________-

a) Time schedule b) Work curve

c) Series of job d) Series of project

149. Which of the following is most suitable for traditional room ______________

a) Pottery b) Brass sculpture

c) Indoor plant d) Paper Mache wall hanging

150. Flat piece of furniture may be placed at______________

a) Right angle b) Obtuse angle

c) Acute angle d) None of the above

151. Primary colours are colours created out of combinations of ______________

a) Red, green, blue b) Red yellow, blue

c) Red, green, yellow d) Red, black, yellow

152. A good kitchen must provide space and equipment for______________

a) Preparation b) Washing

c) Cooking and serving d) All of these

153. Popular type of kitchen and the best layout of the different centres in the kitchen is______________

a) U-shaped kitchen b) Broken U-shaped kitchen

c) L-shaped kitchen d) Broken L shaped

154. Long term goals need a lot of ______________

a) Motivation b) Understanding

c) Skilful direction d) All of these

155. The power of control helps to overcome____________

a) Problems b) Barriers

c) Both a and b d) Coordinate

156. ________________ is the moral value than anything

a) Affection b) Comfort

c) Punctuality d) Beauty

157. Standards measure the amount and degree of ________ received

a) Interest b) Satisfaction

c) Both a and d) Attitude

158. ___________ of the family will greatly influence the standard of living

a) Composition b) Attitude

c) Both a and b d) None of these

159. ________________ refers to the ability to do work

a) Strength b) Energy

c) Health d) None of these

160. ________________ leads to prolonged excessive activity without obtaining sufficient rest

a) Stress b) Fatigue

c) Fever d) All of these

161. The causes of muscular tension is______________

a) Accumulation of lactic acid and carbon dioxide

b) Accumulations of lactic acid

c) Accumulation of carbon dioxide

d) Accumulation of lactic acid and nitrogen

162. Home maker must be conscious about________________

a) Menu planning b) Keeping household clean

c) Time plan d) All of these

163. The energy need is largely determined by______________

a) The stages of life cycle b) The state of mind

c) The state of ill health d) All of these

164. The posture of the body is directly related to the way of ________

a) Carrying body to involve in activities

b) Diet maintaining

c) Gyming

d) All of these

165. Selection of standard is based on ________

a) Fundamental goal b) Comfortable living

c) Satisfaction d) Interest

166. The energy is measured in terms of ________

a) Oxygen consumed by the body

b) Calories consumed by the body

c) Joules consumed by the body

d) None of these

167. Which of the following is/ are true?

a) Age influences the amount of energy expanded

b) Bending requires less energy than reaching

c) Energy spending is influenced by the sequence of activity

d) Both b and c

168. Intense muscular activity demand ________ gas

a) Hydrogen b) Carbon

c) Oxygen d) Nitrogen

169. Aversion of any work leads to________

a) Stress b) Frustration

c) Absent mind d) All of these

170. In intense muscular activity incomplete breakdown of nutrients reduced to ________

a) Lactic acid b) Pyruvic acid

c) Acetic acid d) Oxaloacetic acid

171. The state of giving rest to body and work to hand is called________

a) Motion economy b) Work place arrangement

c) Planning work place d) Rhythmic motion

172. The basic managerial skills are ______

a) To supervise b) To stimulate

c) To motivate d) All of these

173. The final alteration in desirable situation will create______________

a) Minimum satisfaction b) Maximum satisfaction

c) No satisfaction d) None of these

174. Resources like skill and time are classified as______________

a) Human resources b) Material resources

c) Psychological resources d) Shared resource

175. The decision taken during natural calamities is kind of _________

a) Conscious decision b) Routine decision

c) Perfect decision d) Immediate decision

176. Taking care of the children is the example of __________

a) Collective decision b) Immediate decision

c) Personal decision d) Routine decision

177. Which of the following is incorrect?

a) Savings are inversely proportionate to investments

b) Savings is very important from the national point of view

c) Savings are the difference between earning and expenditure

d) Savings represent the provision made at any point of time for use at a later date

178. Which of the following to be considered with choosing the location or site?

a) The surroundings

b) The type of house in the community

c) The desirability of the neighbourhood

d) All of the above

179. What is called to keep the expenditure limited according to the income?

a) Goal b) Planning

c) Budget d) List

180. Bank interest on the money is called ________

a) Debentures b) Loan

c) Advance d) Both a and c

181. ________ is an attractive method of saving for persons in service

a) Provident fund b) Share and debentures

c) Post office saving d) UTI

182. ________ is also called as fixed montage

a) Amortized mort age b) Straight montage

c) Chatter montage d) Promising note

183. Records maintained for income and expenditure helps________

a) To know the way the money is being spent

b) To complete present expenditure with that of the past

c) To balance the budget

d) All of these

184. Which of the following to be considered with choosing the location or site?

a) The surroundings

b) The type of house in the community

c) The desirability of the neighbourhood

d) All of these

185. While constructing a house living room and bedroom should face the ________

a) South b) West

c) Both a and b d) North

186. Combination of ________ gives rise to forms

a) Space b) Line

c) Pattern d) Texture

187. The colour that can be used in masses is ________

a) Red b) Pink

c) Orange d) All of these

188. Common stock holders get ________ dividend lattes

a) High b) Low

c) Very low d) Very high

189. Orange colour is associated with ____________

a) Energy b) Well being

c) Light d) All of these

190. Diagonal lines are suggested for ____________

a) A life and dignity b) Movement and force

c) Grace and flexibility d) Subtle and rich effect

191. The flower vase or pot can be in ____________ shape

a) Spherical b) Round

c) Triangle d) None of the above

192. Which provides sense of restfulness and response?

a) Proportion b) Harmony

c) Light d) Balance

193. Pewter is an alloy of tin with ____________

a) Lead b) Chromium

c) Copper d) Aluminium

194. ________ motifs are destroyed when combined with geometric motifs

a) Naturalistic motifs b) Stylized motifs

c) Both a and b d) None of these

195. Which of the statement is correct?

a) Prangs colour chart system is used in both interior and decorative

b) Certain combination of colour gives a feeling of equilibrium and rhythm

c) Prangs colour chart explain common colour harmonious not used in home decoration

d) Prang colour chart system is hard to understand

196. To arrange the flowers it should be noticed that the ____________ of the flower will attract everyone

a) Colour b) Shape

c) Smell d) Size

197. When red orange and blue purple are combined with yellow green for harmony it is ____________

a) Analogue colour b) Triad colour

c) Complementary colour d) Split complementary

198. In furniture arrangement formal balance tend to appear ________
a) Graceful b) Dull
c) Monotonous d) Stilted

199. Colour scheme for furniture should be planned with________
a) Shape b) Exposure
c) Size d) All of these

200. Which of the following are fundamental of furniture arrangements?
a) Keep accessories in proportion to furniture
b) Keep furniture in proportion to space
c) Arrangement may be symmetrical or asymmetrical
d) All of these

201. Tables and chairs should harmonize in____________
a) Weight b) Style
c) Both a and b d) None of these

202. A side board provides storage space in a ____________ area
a) Living room b) Dining room
c) Bedroom d) Kitchen

203. Judicious use of colour helps to convey the feeling of____________
a) Tranquillity b) Coolness
c) Dignity d) All of these

204. Texture also influences____________________
a) Scale b) Design
c) Focus d) Balance

205. Flowers should be arranged twice the height of the containers in ________________
a) Low b) Tall
c) Narrow d) Shallow

206. Why the surrounding of the house should be clean?
a) To get a light and air b) Maintain good health
c) Keep away from insect d) To keep the bushes clean

207. In flower arrangement unity is used in ____________
a) Flowers with the containers b) Background
c) Position d) All of these

208. Which of the following statement is correct?

a) Leaves and ferns should be used along with foliage

b) Delicate and fine texture should be mixed

c) Light flowers should be used at the focal point

d) Flowers should be cramped

209. To prolong the life of flower ___________ can be added to slow down the bacterial growth

a) Camphor b) Salt

c) Charcoal d) All of these

210. Dried materials such as __________ are used in flower arrangement

a) Wood Rosen b) Wood berries

c) Cones d) All of these

211. Good repellent of cockroaches is ____________

a) Borax b) Kerosene

c) Pyrethrum powder d) All of these

212. Time schedule should be prepared by _______________.

a) Through discussion among the family members

b) According to one's own thinking only

c) According to the habits and abilities of the family members

d) All of these

213. Punctuality and integrity are example of ____________.

a) Ethical values b) Moral values

c) Instrumental values d) None of these

214. Conventional standards are usually associated with __________

a) Tradition b) Customs

c) Social taboos d) All of these

215. Owning a house is example of _______________

a) Short term goal b) Long term goal

c) Intermediate goal d) None of these

216. The stages of family cycle is_______________

a) Beginning family contracting family, expanding family

b) Contracting family, beginning family, expanding family

c) Beginning family, expanding family, contracting family

d) Expanding family, contracting family, beginning family

217. Ironing, climbing stairs are example of _______________

a) Light work b) Moderate work

c) Heavy work d) None of these

218. Peak loads are periods where activities are concentrated_________

a) More in certain periods of time b) Less in certain periods of time

c) More always d) Less always

219. Analysis of smooth and rhythmic movements of an activity is done in_______________

a) Micro motion film analysis b) Cyclograph

c) Chromocyclography d) Process chart

220. Changes at the place of work can be adopted through__________

a) Proper stage place b) Proper equipment

c) Labour saving device d) All of these

221. Looking after the children is example of ____________

a) Personal decision b) Routine decision

c) Collective decision d) None of these

222. The previous experience and learning from the basis of _________

a) Conscious decision b) New decision

c) Immediate decision d) None of these

223. Which of the statement is incorrect?

a) Ownership ties the family to the locality

b) Property values may decline resulting in loss of capital

c) The struggle to meets cost of home ownership may rob the family of other development

d) None of these

224. The aspect or location of the kitchen most favoured is ________

a) East b) West

c) North d) South

225. A beautifully shaped well polished mahogany table needs to be displayed against ________ to achieve harmony

a) Dark background b) Floral prints

c) Light background d) Dark shades

226. In home furnishing, texture may be used in a wider sense and refers to the ________

a) Finish of walls, rugs or other floor coverings

b) Wood work

c) Painting, ceramics

d) Any of these

227. The single most important facto governing the size and composition of the labour for is ________

a) The birth rate b) Population growth

c) The death rate d) Diversity

228. Which of the statement is incorrect?

a) Most furnishing scheme attempt to express a definite idea, a theme or a mood

b) Furnishing excite an emotional response in the viewer and in the user

c) Informal decors the rooms express dignity and reserve and are impressive

d) None of these

229. Tertiary colours are obtained by mixing________

a) Primary colours b) Secondary colours

c) Both a and b d) None of these

230. The use of colours helps to________

a) Contrast b) Blend

c) Accent d) All of these

231. Use of two colours which lie directly opposite to each other on the colour wheel is ___________

a) Complementary colour b) Analogous colour

c) Split complementary colour d) Triad colour

232. Use of three colours to get harmony is_______________

a) Analogous colour harmony b) Triad colour harmony

c) Split complementary harmony d) Monochromatic colour harmony

233. Use of different tint or shades of one hue or colour gives_________

a) Analogous colour harmony

b) Monochromatic colour harmony

c) Split complementary colour harmony

d) Triad colour harmony

234. A suggestive hope is ______

a) Blue b) Purple

c) Brown d) Green

235. Formal balance of furniture arrangements tends to appear______

a) Stilted b) Monotonous

c) Dull d) Graceful

236. Bed room accessories include________________

a) Radio b) TV

c) Dressing table d) All of the above

237. Balance and stability of flower arrangement is __________

a) Virtual b) Actual

c) Lateral d) Both a and b

238. Flat pieces of furniture may be placed at ___________

a) Right angles b) Obtuse angles

c) Acute angles d) None of the above

239. The important aid to flower arrangement is ___________

a) Water b) Pair of scissors

c) Hammer d) Air

240. Flower should be arranged twice the height of the container________

a) Talls b) Low

c) Shallow d) Narrow

241. The input of the family system is______________

a) Met demands
b) Demands and resources
c) Used resources
d) Personal system

242. Silver wares should be washed with______________

a) Soda
b) Ammonia
c) Zinc powder
d) None of the above

243. Human resource management refers to ___________

a) All managerial work
b) Concept and techniques for organizing work activities
c) Management techniques for controlling people at work
d) The management of people in organization

244. The front loading washing machine is also called______________

a) Agitation type
b) Tumbler type
c) Automatic washer
d) Pulsator washes

245. The longest stem in ikebana is______________

a) Shin
b) Tai
c) Soe
d) Earth

246. Wall to wall carpet produces illusion in______________

a) Size
b) Colour
c) Luxury
d) Space

247. Olive green is a ______________

a) Primary colour
b) Secondary colour
c) Tertiary colour
d) Quaternary colour

248. A criteria closely related to structural design is ___________

a) Beauty
b) Durability
c) Functionalism
d) Suitability

249. The ambiguity in a massages denotation or connotation is called______

a) Semantic noise
b) Pragmatic noise
c) Syntactic noise
d) None of the above

250. Walls painted by sunshine yellow colour will bring a feeling of______

a) Coolness
b) Warmth
c) Distan
d) Monotone

Answers

1. d	2. d	3. b	4. b	5. d	6. b	7. b	8. a	9. b	10. d
11. b	12. c	13. b	14. d	15. d	16. c	17. d	18. a	19. a	20. a
21. a	22. d	23. b	24. d	25. d	26. c	27. d	28. a	29. b	30. a
31. a	32. a	33. b	34. c	35. a	36. a	37. c	38. c	39. a	40. d
41. d	42. b	43. B	44. B	45. C	46. C	47. D	48. D	49. C	50. C
51. c	52. a	53. d	54. c	55. d	56. a	57. b	58. b	59. a	60. d
61. d	62. d	63. a	64. a	65. a	66. b	67. d	68. d	69. b	70. b
71. b	72. a	73. b	74. b	75. d	76. c	77. a	78. d	79. b	80. b
81. a	82. a	83. d	84. b	85. a	86. b	87. a	88. a	89. a	90. d
91. b	92. d	93. d	94. d	95. c	96. d	97. b	98. c	99. b	100. d
101. a	102. b	103. d	104. b	105. c	106. a	107. c	108. c	109. b	110. b
111. b	112. d	113. b	114. b	115. b	116. c	117. b	118. c	119. a	120. c
121. b	122. a	123. c	124. b	125. c	126. d	127. c	128. d	129. b	130. d
131. d	132. b	133. d	134. c	135. c	136. c	137. d	138. b	139. b	140. c
141. c	142. d	143. c	144. c	145. d	146. d	147. c	148. a	149. b	150. a
151. B	152. d	153. a	154. d	155. c	156. c	157. d	158. a	159. b	160. b
161. a	162. d	163. a	164. d	165. a	166. a	167. a	168. c	169. d	170. a
171. a	172. d	173. b	174. a	175. d	176. d	177. a	178. d	179. c	180. d
181. a	182. b	183. d	184. d	185. c	186. b	187. b	188. b	189. d	190. b
191. d	192. d	193. a	194. b	195. a	196. a	197. b	198. d	199. d	200. d
201. c	202. b	203. d	204. d	205. b	206. b	207. d	208. a	209. c	210. d
211. d	212. a	213. b	214. d	215. b	216. d	217. b	218. a	219. c	220. d
221. b	222. b	223. d	224. a	225. c	226. d	227. b	228. d	229. c	230. d
231. a	232. b	233. b	234. b	235. a	236. d	237. d	238. a	239. b	240. a
241. b	242. b	243. a	244. b	245. a	246. d	247. d	248. c	249. a	250. c

5

Human Development

1. Child development is defined as a field of study devoted to the understanding of all facts of human growth and development given by ___________

a) Hurlock b) Papivae and olds

c) Harries d) Berk

2. The science of child development deals with_______________

a) Stages of growth and maturation

b) The psychological and social interaction between a child

c) Effect of environment influence up on the individual patterns of development

d) All of these

3. Physical and intellectual growth may be due to_______________

a) Health b) Emotional climate

c) Cultural atmosphere d) All of these

4. The study about different approach in human development is known as__________

a) Cross sectional study b) Longitudinal study

c) Both a and b d) None of the above

5. Factors that influence growth and development of infant is__________

a) Birth injuries and cultural stimulation

b) Nutrition and care of the baby

c) Environment, medical aid and care provided

d) All of these

6. The kind of growth and development observed in child's life is ______

a) Physical b) Emotional

c) Intellectual and social d) All of these

7. Which of these is not an inherited emotion?

a) Emotional reactivity b) Display of feelings

c) Sensation seeking d) All of the above

8. DB stands for__________________.

a) Disruptive Behaviour b) Deficit Behaviour

c) Defiant Behaviour d) All of these

9. CAT stands __________

a) Children's Apperception Test b) Children's Appearance Test

c) Both a & b d) None of these

10. The emerging and expanding of capacities of the individual to provide progressively greater facility in functioning is________________

a) Growth. b) Maturation

c) Development d) None of these

11. Which forms the large part of developmental psychology __________?

a) The study of children's physiology

b) The study of children's behaviour

c) The study of children's food habits

d) The study of children's clothing

12. What does child development concentrate on___________

a) Discovering characteristic on the child

b) Changes in appearance, behavior and interest

c) How the change occur

d) All of these

13. Which of these studied in child psychology________________?

a) Meaning of childhood b) Parental influences

c) Child training methods d) All of these

14. Child psychology is______________

a) Qualitative study of children's behaviour

b) Quantitative study of children's behaviour

c) Qualitative and quantitative study of children's behaviour

d) None of the above

15. Growth refers to ______________

a) Improvement in the functioning of the body processes

b) Process limited to specific area

c) Process that can be easily measured and observed

d) Increase in size , height, and weight etc

16. Birth defects or abnormalities are called as

a) Congenital defects b) Intranatal defects

c) Post natal defects d) Labour defects

17. Differences in the pattern of physical and intellectual growth may be due to __________

a) Health b) Emotional climate

c) Cultural atmosphere d) All of the above

18. Freudian psycho analysis is the most prominent in__________

a) Trait theory b) Motivational theory

c) Social behavioral theory d) All of these

19. In childhood the weight gain principally comes from__________

a) Bone b) Muscle tissue

c) Both a and b d) None of the above

20. In adult gain in weight is from __________

a) Accumulation of fat tissue b) Lack of activity

c) Blood d) Hormones

21. Which of the following is /are true__________

a) ADHD can be treated with drugs

b) Medical psychological, educational intervention and behavioral management are integral treatment for ADHD

c) Both a and b

d) None of the above

22. DTaP vaccine is against which infectious disease__________

a) Diphtheria b) Tetanus

c) Pertussis d) All of the above

23. The cause of phobia could be____________

a) Classical conditioning b) Social

c) Emotional d) All of these

24. Thematic Apperception Test developed at____________

a) Harvard University b) NIN

c) NSI d) WHO

25. Which of these is considered as intellectual development ________

a) Abilities in memory, imagination, language

b) Abilities in percept's and concepts

c) Problem solving abilities

d) All of these

26. The child's reaction and response to other people depends on________

a) Social learning b) Experience provided

c) Behavioural models provided d) All of these

27. Birth to one year of life is known as____________

a) Childhood b) Infancy

c) Adolescence d) None of these

28. Imaginative thinking occur at the age of____________

a) 12 years b) 9 years

c) 6 years d) 3 years

29. The union department of social welfare was created in the year of __________

a) 1964 b) 1954

c) 1946 d) 1945

30. FED stands for____________

a) Feeding and Eating Disorders

b) Feeling and Emotional Disorders

c) Both a and b

d) None of these

31. Socialization teaches the child

a) How to control his emotions b) How to hide his emotions

c) How to express his emotions d) None of the above

32. Dyslexia can be identified among child at the age of ______

a) Two years b) Three years

c) Four years d) Five years

33. CSWB stands for ______

a) Central Social Welfare Board

b) Central Society of Welfare Board

c) Central Scheme of Welfare Board

d) None of these

34. State social welfare advisory board act as the counterparts of______

a) CSNB b) SWRD

c) DSW d) None of these

35. Central social welfare board was set up in the year of ______

a) 1969 b) 1953

c) 1979 d) 1973

36. Condensed course of education for adult women was started by______

a) SWB b) CSWB

c) SWRD d) All of these

37. Mahila Mandals, a women's organisation receives grants from______

a) SWB b) CSWB

c) Both a and b d) None of these

38. Language of word is not necessary for ______

a) Imaginative thinking b) Conceptual thinking

c) Associate thinking d) Perceptual thinking

39. Which of these are associated with insecurely attached infants in later life?

a) Less competent b) has less mature friends

c) Less socially skilled d) All of the above

40. At birth there is only one primitive kind of emotion which is______

a) Sorrow b) Loneliness

c) State of general excitation d) Fear

41. The period of 4 years to 6 years in the development of a child is known as________.
   a) Early childhood b) Later childhood
   c) Boy hood and girlhood d) None of these

42. The period of 8-12 years in the development of child is known as________
   a) Later childhood b) Boy hood and girl hood
   c) Adolescence d) None of these

43. Later child hood is a phase where________________
   a) Physical growth is not as rapid
   b) The child tent to be restless
   c) The child grows stronger and steadier and should be kept well occupied
   d) All of these

44. The expected development of child hood is ______________
   a) Learning to walk, talk and take solid food
   b) Learning sex difference and sexual modesty
   c) Achieving physiological stability
   d) All of these

45. The period of complete dependence is____________________
   a) Early child hood b) Late child hood
   c) Infancy d) None of these

46. What is necessary for optimum growth and development ________?
   a) Proper medical care timely
   b) Immunization and early diagnosis
   c) Cure of deficiency and disease
   d) All of these

47. Factors influencing child development are____________
   a) Psychological factors
   b) Family culture and social set up
   c) Rest and exercise
   d) All of these

48. Tetany is caused by the malfunctioning of ___________
   a) Thyroid gland b) Parathyroid gland
   c) Pituitary gland d) Adrenal gland

49. Malfunctioning of islets of langerhans result in_____________-
    a) Tremors, breathing problem
    b) Decreased resistance to infection
    c) Diabetes
    d) All of these
50. Addison's disease, sexual abnormalities etc., affecting growth and development is caused by malfunctioning of_____________
    a) Parathyroid gland b) Thyroid gland
    c) Adrenal gland d) Islets of langerhans
51. ICDS stands for________________
    a) Integrated Child Development Services
    b) Integrated Child Development Scheme
    c) International Child Development Services
    d) India Child Development Scheme
52. ICDS programme implemented through__________
    a) State government b) Union territories
    c) Both a and b d) None of these
53. ICDS package includes___________________
    a) Supplementary Nutrition b) Health check up
    c) Immunization d) All of the above
54. Malfunctioning of sex glands or gonads results in_____________
    a) Pre mature sexual development
    b) Late sexual development
    c) Lots of tension and frustration
    d) All of these
55. Physical and mental development of an individual is largely dependent on the efficient working of__________________
    a) Respiratory organs b) Endocrine glands
    c) Other glands d) None of the above
56. Dwarfism, gigantism, abnormalities in learning and adjustment may be the cause of abnormal____________________
    a) Thyroid gland b) Pituitary gland
    c) Para thyroid gland d) None of the above

57. Thyroxin is manufactured by__________

a) Parathyroid gland b) Thyroid gland

c) Adrenal gland d) None of these

58. To get a complete picture of an individual you must understand how__________

a) Children develop physically

b) Children develop psychologically

c) Children develop physically and psychologically

d) None of these

59. FCH stand for__________

a) Foster Care Homes b) Foster Care House

c) Faster Care Homes d) None of these

60. How many foster care homes situated in India__________

a) 4 b) 3

c) 5 d) 2

61. Foster care homes funded by__________

a) ICDS b) WHO

c) CSWB d) SWB

62. The aspect of development that influence behaviour directly or indirectly is__________

a) Motor development b) Emotional development

c) Physical development d) Cognitive development

63. Cognitive development in the elementary school year is __________

a) Systematic b) Rational

c) Predictable d) All of these

64. Changes regulated by inner time clock refers to __________

a) Learning b) Maturation

c) Growth d) Guidance

65. Between conception and birth, the period of first two week is called as __________.

a) Embryonic period b) Germinal period

c) Foetal period d) None of these

66. The condition of pregnancy can usually be confirmed by a laboratory test called ______________.

a) Squirrel test | b) Mouse or rabbit test
c) Hamster test | d) None of these

67. Embryonic period lasts for about______________

a) 2 weeks | b) 8weeks
c) 4weeks | d) None of these

68. For well adjusted childhood, a child______________

a) Must have carefree adulthood
b) Should be kept at minimum unpleasant emotions
c) All of these
d) None of these

69. Morality means______________

a) Conforming to social standards vulnerability
b) Conforming to mental standards vulnerability
c) Conforming to physical standards vulnerability
d) None of these

70. The embryo measures about ¼" to 2" long in______________

a) Germinal period | b) Embryonic period
c) Foetal period | d) None of these

71. Prenatal period is ______________

a) The first 4 weeks after conception
b) The entire term between conception and birth
c) The last 4 weeks before conception
d) None of these

72. The fluid that fills the sac in which the embryo is present is called______________

a) Amniotic fluid | b) Neurotic fluid
c) Biotic fluid | d) None of these

73. The embryo gets nourishment through the umbilical cord from______________

a) Amniotic fluid | b) Placenta
c) Neurotic fluid | d) None of these

74. During 2nd month of pregnancy the embryo is________

a) About 1 cm long b) About 1 mm long

c) About 1inch long d) None of these

75. A baby born is____________ days from conception

a) 340 b) 280

c) 240 d) 380

76. During pregnancy a women's basal metabolism goes up by________

a) 5%-10% b) 10%-20%

c) 20%-30% d) 40%-50%

77. During normal labour, which part of the baby comes out first______

a) Hand b) Leg

c) Head d) None of these

78. The process of child birth is called as________

a) Gestation b) Labour

c) Conception d) None of these

79. The child birth is divided in to__________

a) 2 stages b) 3 stages

c) 4 stages d) 5 stages

80. For a pregnant women, a good balanced diet about__________

a) 1000-2000 kcal /day b) 2500-3000kcal/day

c) 4000-5000 kcal/day d) None of these

81. Ante partum haemorrhage is the bleeding from the vagina________

a) During pregnancy b) After birth

c) CLEFT palate d) None of these

82. Common birth defect is____________

a) Mongolism, b) Haemophilia

c) CREFT palate, d) Colour blindness

83. A clean cut on the floor of the pelvis rather than a tear to favour labour is called __________

a) Angiosiotomy b) Vaginosiotomy

c) Episiotomy d) None of the above

84. Antepartum haemorrhage is usually due to__________

a) Threaten miscarriage b) Placenta praenia

c) Detachment of after birth d) All of the above

85. The cause of infant and child mortality might be due to__________

a) Poor nutrition& poor public awareness

b) Infectious disease&poor medical facilities

c) Poor education of parents& regarding child care

d) Any of these

86. Neonatal mortality might be due to__________

a) Premature birth

b) Birth injuries &infectious disease

c) Congenital deformities

d) Any of these

87. The baby after delivery sometimes is held down upside and slapped to__________.

a) Help start normal breathing

b) Throw out secretions in the mouth and nose

c) Clear up the air passage

d) All of these

88. Agalactia may be due to __________

a) Anaemia

b) Mal nutrition, emotional disturbance

c) Bearing children at very late or very early age

d) Any of these

89. An infection of umbilical cord in new born means__________

a) The cord remains wet and does not fall

b) The cord has a foul smell

c) The area around the cord is red and swollen

d) All of these

90. After the birth a baby to be examined, cleaned and weighed with special attention towards__________

a) The cord and genitals

b) The head and external organs

c) The bones& internal organs

d) All of these

91. A premature baby ____________
    a) Does not have fully developed organ system
    b) Difficulties in feeding and breathing
    c) No resistance to disease & get affected with cold quickly
    d) Has all the above mentioned complications

92. The baby cuts first molar teeth at usually____________
    a) 0-2 months b) 4-6 months
    c) 6-12 months d) 18-24 months

93. Hard bulky motion which is difficult to pass is called ________
    a) Constipation b) Diarrhoea
    c) Intestinal disorders d) None of these

94. The baby at 0-2 months has a height of about____________
    a) 10-12 inches b) 12-16 inches
    c) 16-18 inches d) 18-20 inches

95. The scheme for service of children was formulated by________
    a) Department of social welfare
    b) Department of central social welfare board
    c) Department of state social welfare
    d) Department of social welfare and advisory board

96. Welfare extension projects was launched for____________
    a) Rural b) Urban
    c) Both a and b d) None of these

97. Socio economic programme started by____________
    a) Central social welfare board
    b) Central scheme of social welfare board
    c) Central social defense programme
    d) Central welfare extension projects

98. Welfare extension projects was launched in the year of ________
    a) 1955 b) 1958
    c) 1956 d) 1959

99. Socio economic programme started in the year of____________
    a) 1956 b) 1957
    c) 1958 d) 1959

100. Diarrhoea in baby may be due to__________

a) Unclean bottle b) Impure water

c) Unclean teat d) Any of these

101. The action taken during the diarrhoeal illness of the baby __________

a) Doctor should be called at once

b) Boiled, cooled water should be given frequently

c) Boil and keep clean all things to used for the baby

d) All of these

102. Acute pain in the stomach is called__________

a) Cramps b) Flatulence

c) Gastritis d) Colic

103. Loss of colour, twitching muscle of the face, eyes and fingers are the symptoms of__________

a) Thrush b) Advanced diarrhoea

c) Convulsions d) None of these

104. High temperature in an infant may be due to__________

a) Indigestion b) An awkward tooth

c) A cold or onset of illness d) Any of the above

105. Thrush is__________

a) Formation of small spots on the body

b) Small spots on tongue

c) Small spots on the wall of mouth

d) Both b and c

106. Growth proceeding from mass to specific activities is called

a) Integration b) Cephalocaudal sequence

c) Differentiation d) Proximodistial sequence

107. Treatment of colic in infant's is__________

a) Swaddle him snugly in a blanket

b) Put a warm water bottle on infants belly

c) A gentle massage

d) All of the above

108. Flatulence in the baby is probably due to____________

a) Gulping milk too quickly

b) Sucking from an empty breast or bottle

c) Due to intense hunger

d) Any of the above

109. Rickets can be cured or treated by____________

a) Vitamin D b) Calcium

c) Exposure to sun ligh d) All of these

110. The condition of being resistant to a disease is called____________

a) Immunity b) Immunization

c) Resistance d) None of these

111.Antigen is the____________

a) Get substance from the germs carry

b) Protein substance from the germs carry

c) Substance produced by the human body

d) None of these

112. Antibody is the ____________

a) Get substance from the germs carry

b) Protein substance from the germs carries

c) Substance produced by the human body to fight infections

d) None of these

113. The children's act 1960 has been enacted

a) National Institute of Public Co-operation and Child Development

b) Nutritional Institute of Public Co-operation and Child Development

c) National Institute of Public Corporation and Child Development

d) National Institute of Public Corporation and Child Development

115. The aim of human right is ____________

a) To protect human dignity and security

b) To improve human dignity and security

c) To analysis human dignity and security

d) All of these

116. Language development occurs during ____________

a) Sensory motor period b) Germinal period

c) Embryonic period d) Foetal period

117. Central social welfare board was set up in____________

a) March 1953 b) August 1953

c) May 1953 d) June 1953

118. Infant Mortality Rate(IMR) is measured by____________

a) Annual Number of Deaths of Babies Under Two Year ×100
Total live births in a year

b) Annual Number of Morbidity Babies Under Two Year ×100
Total live births in a year

c) Annual Number of Deaths of Babies Under One Year ×1000
Total live births in a year

d) Annual Number of Morbidity of Babies Under One Year ×1000
Total live births in a year

119. Bilingualism is a type of ____________

a) Comprehension defect b) ENT defect

c) Hearing defect d) Speech defect

120. MMR stands for____________

a) Mental mortality rate b) Maternal mortality rate

c) Both a and d) None of these

121. TT stands for ____________

a) Typhoid b) Tetanus

c) Tuberculosis d) None of these

122. While children talk for their own enjoyment, they are using____________

a) Egocentric speech b) Socialized speech

c) Both a and b d) None of these

123. Measles vaccine is usually given to babies'____________ old

a) 3-6 months b) 6-9 months

c) 9-15 months d) None of these

124. Bacille Calmette Guerin (BCG) vaccine against ____________

a) Diphtheria b) Whooping cough

c) Tetanus d) Tuberculosis

125. Oral Polio vaccines (OPV) is against____________

a) Tb

b) Small box

c) Poliomyelitis

d) None of these

126. Fourth and Fifth dose of OPV is given during ________ period of infancy
   a) 4th week later
   b) 8th week later
   c) 3 months later
   d) One year later

127. In the body, gain in weight comes partly from increase in________
   a) Neutral
   b) Glandular
   c) Muscle tissue
   d) All of these

128. Identical twins have____________________
   a) Same genetic make up
   b) Different genetic make up
   c) Both a and b
   d) None of these

129. The anatomical feature of the infant human skull comprising any of the soft membranous gaps between the cranial bones that make up the calvaria is called as_______________
   a) Fontanels
   b) Sutures
   c) Both a and b
   d) None of these

130. Measles will commonly occur in a child during ____________ old
   a) 25 months
   b) 20 months
   c) 30 months
   d) 35 months

131. The heart rate of the new born infants' is__________
   a) 120-140 beats/min
   b) 120-130 beats/mis
   c) 120-150 beats/min
   d) 120-160 beats/min

132. The level of blood pressure to the new born infant is__________mm of Hg

a) 100/60

b) 75/50

c) 65/50

d) 75/65

133. Muscle tissue makes up___________ % of the infants weight at birth

a) 30-40

b) 20-25

c) 40-50

d) 50-70

134. Attachment theories are___________

a) Learning theory

b) Psychoanalytic sub theory

c) Ethological theory

d) All of these

135. The body and brain grow after the process is called__________

a) Development

b) Maturation

c) Behaviour

d) None of these

136. Middle childhood extends from the age of______

a) 10 years

b) 8 years

c) 6 years

d) 4 years

137. Girls show faster growth than the boys of same age during______________

a) Adolescence

b) Early childhood

c) Later childhood

d) None of these

138. The raw material of thinking is ________

a) Symbols
b) Semantics
c) Man
d) Child

139. The period of complete dependence is ________

a) Later childhood
b) Early childhood
c) Infancy
d) All of these

140. Which of the following reflexes are related to feeding ________

a) The Moto and rooting reflexes
b) The rooting and sucking reflexes
c) The Moto and sucking reflexes
d) The babinski and orienting reflexes

141. The advantage of longitudinal studies does not depend on ________

a) Observer
b) Memories
c) Time schedule
d) None

142. Proximodistal means ________

a) From the head to the toes
b) From the past to the future
c) From the centre of the body to the extremities
d) From birth to death

143. The physical and mental factors that affect the development of the child refers to ________

a) Environment
b) Friends
c) Neighbourhood
d) Family

144. Which of the following is not a characteristic of a protestant work ethic?

a) Hard work
b) Do not value leisure
c) spend a lot of money
d) none of the above

145. A person believes in himself and what he stands for, we may call this ________

a) Self extension
b) Self feeling
c) Self objectification
d) Self consistency

146. The trait is said to be ________

a) Common to all
b) In consistency of an individual
c) Distinctive of an individual
d) All of the above

147. Which of following states that different motivates are predominant in the child at different stages of growth ________
a) Theory of personality of dynamics
b) Theory of psycho sexual development
c) Theory of structure of personality
d) None of these

148. The development of moral ideas goes hand in hand with ________
a) Motor development
b) Physical development
c) Cognitive development
d) None of these

149. As a child grows the perception of a child is influenced by ________
a) Personal factor
b) Social factor
c) Cultural factor
d) All of the above

150. Bleeding from vagina immediately after the child birth is called ________
a) Lochia
b) Sochia
c) Fochia
d) All of these

151. In which of the following Praget's theory underestimates the importance ________
a) Cognitive abilities
b) Importance of language
c) Importance of social interactions
d) All of the above

152. Mental age can be found out using ________
a) Growth chart
b) Intelligence test
c) Both a and b
d) None of these

153. Passive play is ________
a) A reading
b) Looking at comics
c) Watching TV
d) All of these

154. The child who makes up to social expectations is the
a) Child who makes good personal adjustments
b) Child who makes good social adjustments
c) Both a and b
d) None of these

155. Strong ammonia smell of the urine is called ________

a) Soreness of buttocks b) Nappy rash

c) Colic d) None of the above

156. Secondary socialization has its beginning at ________

a) Late childhood b) Adolescence

c) Infancy d) Adult

157. Children are prone to illness due to ________

a) Poor pre-natal psychological environment

b) Unfavorable psychological environment

c) Emotional deprivation

d) All of these

158. Faulty eating habits of children elicited with parents ignorance may leads to ____.

a) Under nutrition b) Over nutrition

c) Mal nutrition d) None of these

159. The possibility of a child to be born physically challenged may be due to ______.

a) Heredity factors and unfavorable prenatal environment

b) Series illness of mother during pregnancy

c) Injuries to child during or after birth

d) Any of these

160. Upset in body haemostasis can be caused due to ________

a) Unfavorable physical conditions

b) Unfavorable psychological conditions

c) Unfavorable physical and psychological conditions

d) Unfavorable environmental conditions

161. Upset in haemostasis is due to ________

a) Dwarfism

b) Abnormal B.P.

c) Overweight and underweight problems

d) All of these

162. Too little supervision, over protective activity of adults, lack of emotional controls may all leads to ________

a) Haemostasis b) Mal nutrition

c) Accidents d) Physical handicaps

163. The development of control body movements through the coordinated activity of the body centres, nerves and muscles is called________

a) Sensory development b) Physical development

c) Motor development d) Cognitive development

164. Haemostasis is achieved by the regulatory action of ________

a) Autonomic nervous system b) Endocrine system

c) Both a and b d) None of these

165. A child can walk well enough to balance on a plank when________

a) He is 2 years old
b) He is less than 2 years old
c) He is between 5th and 6th year
d) None of these

166. Factors that facilitate children's learning of skill is________

a) Liability of children's body
b) Fewer previously learnt skills acting as hindrance
c) Curiosity
d) All of these

167. Which of the following is a way to measure activity level in an infant?

a) How often they smile
b) How much they sleep
c) how much they want to be held
d) none of the above

168. Which of the statement is incorrect?

a) The development of motor skills depends on the extent to which opportunity is provided to practice these skills
b) If parents are over protective children will not find difficulty in mastering motor skills
c) More liable parents and teacher find their children inferior in motor skill learning
d) None of these

169. Intelligence test measure ________
   a) Operationally defined intelligence
   b) Quantitative intelligence
   c) Qualitative intelligence
   d) None of these
170. Person's potential for profiting from a certain type of training is called ________
   a) Attitude b) Ability
   c) Aptitude d) None of these
171. Structure of intellect was frame worked by ________
   a) Thurston b) Guilford
   c) Spearman d) Sigmund
172. The two factor theory of intelligence was proposed by ________
   a) Thurstor b) Guilford
   c) Charles Spearman d) Freud
173. Seven primary abilities was identified by ________
   a) Guilford b) Spearman
   c) Thurston d) All port
174. The ability to find rules principles on concept of understanding or solving of problem is called as ________
   a) Space visualization b) Reasoning
   c) Perceptional speed d) One of these
175. Creativity involves________
   a) Deductive thinking b) Inductive thinking
   c) Evaluative thinking d) None of these
176. To get a creative thinker we need to know ________
   a) The kind of thinking that characterize a person
   b) His score on an intelligence test
   c) Both thinking and score on an intelligence test
   d) None of these
177. A creative person's uses ________
   a) Convergent thinking b) Divergent thinking
   c) Both a and b d) None of these

178. Variety of thoughts involved in___________

a) Convergent thinking b) Divergent thinking

c) Both a and b d) None of these

179. The steps involved in thinking of outstanding creative thinker have been studied through ___________

a) Interviews b) Questionnaires

c) Introspection d) All of these

180. The five stages in thinking of outstanding creative thinker in sequence are ___________________

a) Preparation , illumination, evaluation, revision and incubation

b) Preparation, incubation, illumination, evaluation and revision

c) Incubation, preparation, illumination, revision and evaluation

d) None of these

181. Creativity depends on ___________

a) Originality of the person

b) Individual reaction to his originality

c) Society's reaction to his originality

d) All of the above

182. Cognition means _________

a) To know, perceive and understand

b) To express, act and realize

c) To implement and evaluate

d) All of the above

183. Skills like analysis, synthesis, reasoning, comparison, evaluation are ________

a) Motor skills b) Cognitive skills

c) Physical skills d) None of these

184. Which of the statement is incorrect?

a) Perception is selective in nature

b) The child skill is fully developed by the time when the child is 5-6 year of age

c) More the sense is involved the better is perception

d) None of these

185. The stage of problem solving in sequence of ___________

a) Preparation, judgement , production

b) Preparation , production , judgement

c) Judgments , preparation , production

d) Judgments , production , preparation

186. The stages of cognitive development was given ___________

a) Spearman b) Hurlock

c) Piaget d) Allport

187. The quality of understanding is influenced by ___________

a) Condition of sense organs b) Opportunity to learn

c) Type of experiences d) All of the above

188. According to Piaget, there are ___________ stages of intellectual cognitive development

a) 2 b) 3

c) 4 d) 5

189. Which of the statement is incorrect?

a) Learning depends on maturation

b) Maturation depends on learning

c) Individual differs in the learning abilities

d) Learning is a change emerging from an encounter with a situation

190. Psychosomatic disorders are explained by sylee is called ___________

a) General syndrome

b) General adoption syndrome

c) Psycho syndrome

d) Psychosomatic syndrome

191. Fear in children can be reduced by ___________

a) Deliberate diversion of attention and explaining and assuring the children

b) Avoiding compulsion in acquaintance of child

c) Reconditioning the child

d) All of these

192. Jealousy in children can be reduced by ______

a) Reducing parental favouritism

b) Comparison on of one child with another

c) Increasing self confident of the child

d) All of these

193. Which of the statement is incorrect?

a) Bed wetting is known to run in families

b) Bed wetting can be stopped by altering the drinking habits of the child

c) Usually bed wetting ceases by itself as the child grows up

d) Bed wetting is not an emotional problem

194. How will you deal with an emotional child ______?

a) Practice deep breathing b) Identify mood boosters

c) Count to calm down d) All of the above

195. Which of the following is the base of real speech ______?

a) Crying b) Gestures

c) Babbling d) Emotional expressions

196. Most common reason for delayed speech is ______

a) Low grade intelligence

b) Lack of motivation

c) Limited opportunities to practice

d) All of these

197. Crying, babbling, gestures and emotional expression of children are ______

a) Speech forms of communication

b) Pre speech forms of communication

c) Child forms of communication

d) None of these

198. The speech adapted to the behaviour or speech of person to whom the individual is speaking is called as ______

a) Egocentric speech

b) Socialized speech

c) Both a and b

d) None of these

199. Children learning to associate meanings with sound are ________

a) Sentence forming b) Vocabulary building

c) Utterance d) None of these

200. Learning to speak involved ________

a) Learning to utter words b) Building a vocabulary

c) Forming sentence d) All of the above

201. Which of the following is the first task in learning to speak ________

a) Learning to utter words b) Building a vocabulary

c) Forming sentence d) None of these

202. Speech disorders differ from defective speech in the fact that ________

a) They are not caused by faulty learning

b) They can develop at any time during life span

c) They can't be corrected by merely learning correct pronunciations

d) All of these

203. Language and pronunciation are acquired by the child through ________

a) Suggestion b) Imitation

c) Identification d) Competence

204. Jumping or playing with ball, singing, running is form of ________

a) Active play b) Passive play

c) Both a and b d) None of these.

205. The period of "Strom and Stress" thought to be period of ________

a) Early childhood b) Later child hood

c) Adolescence d) Adult hood

206. Which of the statement is incorrect?

a) Children's gangs are play groups

b) Members of children's gangs are of the different sex

c) Most children's gangs have in sigma of belonging

d) To belong a children's gang child must be invited

207. The earliest form of play consisting of things such as kicking, bouncing, wigging, moving fingers and toes etc., is ______________

a) Exploratory play b) Make-believe play

c) Sensor motor play d) Amusements

208. The life span of 40-60 years is the stage of ______________

a) Early adult hood b) Middle age

c) Old age d) None of these

209. Which of the following is a time of free radical adjustments and plateau in development and a hazardous period ______________

a) Early childhood b) Infancy

c) Later childhood d) Adolescence

210. For __________ post natal life, all infants show relatively disorganized behaviour

a) First week b) First 5 days

c) First two days d) First two weeks

211. The baby measures between 23 and 24 inches at ______________

a) 4 months b) 7 months

c) 9 months d) 12 months

212. The baby measures between 28 and 30 inches at ______________

a) 5 months b) 7 months

c) 12 months d) 18 months

213. Which of the following is the shortest of all developmental periods ______________

a) Adolescence b) Early childhood

c) Infancy d) None of these

214. The period from birth to fifteen to thirty minutes after birth is called ______________

a) Period of the neonate b) Period of partunate

c) Period of the maturate d) None of these

215. IQ is ______________

a) Intelligence quota b) Intellectual quota

c) Intelligence quotient d) Intellectual quotient

216. IQ is ______________

a) MA /CA x 100　　b) CA/MA x 100

c) MA/CA x1000　　d) CA/ MA x 1000

217. EQ is ___________

a) Emotional Quotient　　b) Emotional Quota

c) Empathy Quotient　　d) Empathy Quota

218. The developmental task during infancy is ___________

a) Learning to take solid food

b) Learning physical skills

c) Achieving mature relations with age mates

d) Developing concepts

219. The developmental task during late childhood is ___________

a) Learning to walk

b) Learning to gets along with age mates

c) Preparing for an economic carrier

d) Learning to talk

220. A record of a child's behaviour for a stated period of time is ___________

a) Dairy record　　b) Anecdotal record

c) Self report　　d) Assessment report

221. The developmental task during adolescence is ___________

a) Getting ready to read

b) Achieving personal independence

c) Preparing for marriage and family life

d) Selecting a mate

222. TAT is ___________

a) Thematic Apperception Test

b) Theoretical Apperception Test

c) Timely Apperception Test

d) Toddler Apperception Test

223. A widely used projection test of personality in which individuals are asked to describe what they see in a series of inkblots ________

a) Inventory b) Self- report

c) Rorschach tests d) None

224. Which of the following would be evolved traits?

a) Tendency to over eat

b) Quick response to danger

c) Aggression in men

d) All of the above

225. The Rorschach test developed by the Swiss psychiatrist Hermann Rorschach in the year ________

a) 1910s b) 1920s

c) 1930s d) 1940s

226. Which of the statement is incorrect?

a) Play can satisfy a child's desires

b) Play allow to release of pent up emotions

c) Play helps in developing a realistic self concept

d) Play does not make children to learn sex role

227. Which of the statement is incorrect?

a) Play helps physical growth of a child

b) Play develop a child social skills

c) Play helps in healthy personality development

d) Play does not a encourage a child to speak and communicate

228. According to ________ Free and spontaneous play is an important activity for a child

a) Maria Montessori b) Froebel

c) Hurlock d) None of these

229. Painting is an example of ________

a) 2 dimensional hard work

b) 3 dimensional work

c) Both a and b

d) None of these

230. The embryo gets nourishment through the umbilical cord from

a) Aminotic fluid b) Placenta

c) Neurotic fluid d) None of these

231. Puppet is an example of ______________

a) 2 dimensional hard work b) 3 dimensional work

c) Both a and b d) None of these

232. Toys must be ______________

a) Unbreakable b) Without sharp edges

c) Not highly mechanized d) All of these

233. Social institution governed by cultural norms ______________

a) Society b) Family

c) Both a and b d) None of these

234. Joint family ______________

a) Allows division of labour

b) Has greater economy and expenditure per member

c) Offers more time for leisure and recreation

d) Provides all these

235. Grand parents can ______________

a) Influence a family's relationship positively

b) Influence a family's relationship negatively

c) Both depending on the role they tent to play

d) None of these

236. In late child hood ______________

a) School and home should provide conducive environment for development

b) Hearing situation should be organized

c) All available sources should be used to develop a child

d) All of the above are necessary

237. Which of the statement is incorrect?

a) Breast feeding prevents breast cancer

b) Morbidity and mortality rate of breast fed infants is lower than that of bottle fed infants

c) Need for sucking is fully satisfied in breast feeding and thumb sucking is less common

d) None of these

238. Which of the statement is incorrect?

a) Immunity against typhoid is produced by injecting dead typhoid bacteria

b) Small pox vaccine contains living viruses

c) It may take several weeks following an injection for the body to build up effective immunity

d) At birth, there are no antibodies present in a new born baby

239. Triple antigen protects against ________

a) Tetanus, whooping, diphtheria

b) Whooping cough, diarrhoea, polio

c) Diphtheria, salmonellosis, hepatitis

d) Pertusis, tetanus , typhoid

240. Fear in children can be reduced by ________

a) Deliberate diversion of attention and explaining and assuring the children

b) Avoiding compulsion in acquaintance of child

c) Reconditioning the child

d) All of these

241. Which of the statement is incorrect?

a) Fears learned either by direct association

b) Young children are not afraid of more things than either babies or older children

c) Fear can do a lot of harm to the child's development and success in life

d) None of these

242. Which of the statement is incorrect?

a) Cognitive development and mental growth run parallel to each other

b) Language skill, mental ability, relationships are common to both intelligence and cognitive ability

c) For a child who is slow to pick up, it is advisable to provide repetition experience to help him to clarify the concepts

d) Cognitive abilities do not develop with age

243. Setting goal for children will make ___________

a) Children develop a realistic self concept which is healthy for one's development

b) Children develop favorable self concept

c) Children develop a correct self insight

d) None of these

244. If a child aggressive and learns that this behaviour makes him unpopular, he ___________

a) Curl is aggressiveness and change his behaviour and becomes friendly

b) Feels vindictive of the people around him

c) Goals recluse

d) Becomes more aggressive

245. Which of the following is necessary for proper development of speaking skills?

a) Physical readiness and mental readiness to speak

b) Motivation and guidance

c) A good model to imitate and opportunities for practice

d) All of these

246. The large part of the developmental psychology is called ___________

a) The study of children food habits

b) The study of children's clothing

c) The study of children's physiology

d) The study of children's behaviour

247. Behavioural abnormalities in children are identified by ___________

a) Lying b) Fearing

c) Annoying d) All of these

248. Some children are more active than others from birth. This may be due to

a) Environment factors b) Hereditary factors

c) Psychological factors d) Social factors

249. Haemorrhage, sepsis, anaesthesia are example of ____________

a) Non obstetric causes of maternal mortality

b) Obstetric causes of maternal mortality

c) Both a and b

d) None of these

250. The period in which the fertilized egg develops by a process of cell division with hallow sphere of cell is known as ____________

a) Embryonic period b) Germinal period

c) Foetal period d) None of these

Answers

1. d	2. c	3. a	4. a	5. d	6. a	7. d	8. a	9. a	10. d
11. b	12. d	13. d	14. c	15. a	16. a	17. d	18. b	19. a	20. a
21. c	22. d	23. a	24. a	25. c	26. a	27. b	28. d	29. a	30. a
31. c	32. a	33. a	34. a	35. b	36. a	37. b	38. a	39. d	40. c
41. a	42. b	43. d	44. d	45. c	46. c	47. d	48. b	49. c	50. c
51. a	52. c	53. a	54. d	55. b	56. b	57. b	58. c	59. a	60. b
61. c	62. c	63. d	64. b	65. b	66. b	67. b	68. c	69. b	70. a
71. b	72. a	73. b	74. c	75. b	76. a	77. c	78. b	79. b	80. b
81. a	82. d	83. c	84. d	85. d	86. d	87. d	88. d	89. d	90. b
91. d	92. c	93. a	94. d	95. b	96. a	97. a	98. b	99. c	100. d
101. d	102. c	103. c	104. c	105. d	106. c	107. d	108. d	109. d	110. a
111. b	112. c	113. a	114. a	115. a	116. a	117. b	118. c	119. d	120. a
121. b	122. b	123. c	124. d	125. c	126. a	127. d	128. b	129. c	130. a
131. c	132. a	133. b	134. a	135. b	136. b	137. b	138. a	139. b	140. c
141. b	142. c	143. d	144. c	145. b	146. c	147. b	148. c	149. d	150. a
151. d	152. c	153. d	154. c	155. d	156. a	157. d	158. c	159. d	160. c
161. d	162. c	163. c	164. c	165. c	166. d	167. b	168. a	169. a	170. c
171. b	172. c	173. c	174. b	175. b	176. a	177. c	178. c	179. d	180. b
181. d	182. d	183. b	184. b	185. b	186. c	187. b	188. c	189. b	190. b
191. d	192. c	193. d	194. d	195. c	196. d	197. b	198. b	199. b	200. d
201. b	202. d	203. b	204. a	205. c	206. b	207. c	208. b	209. b	210. c

211. a	212. c	213. c	214. b	215. c	216. a	217. a	218. a	219. b	220. a
221. b	222. a	223. c	224. d	225. b	226. d	227. d	228. a	229. a	230. d
231. b	232. d	233. b	234. d	235. c	236. d	237. d	238. d	239. a	240. d
241. b	242. c	243. a	244. a	245. d	246. d	247. d	248. b	249. b	250. d

6

Food Service Management

1. Job description should not be ________.
   a) Clear cut
   b) Brief
   c) Local language
   d) Mother tongue
2. ________ is most important for the success of any establishment.
   a) Individual goals subordinate to establishment goals
   b) Performance and efficiency
   c) Multidirectional goals subordinate to establishment goals
   d) All
3. A rectangular kitchen is built for ________.
   a Hotels
   b) Schools
   c) Hospitals
   d) Catering
4. The foodservice system in which food is purchased all along the food processing continuum, prepared and held either chilled or frozen, and served on-site is called ________.
   a) Ready-prepared
   b) Conventional
   c) Centralized
   d) Assembly-serve
5. Equipment is classified according to ________.
   a) Weight of size
   b) Order of use
   c) Mode of operation
   d) All of these
6. One of the major advantages of process-oriented layouts is ________.
   a) High equipment utilization
   b) Smooth and continuous flow of work
   c) Flexibility in equipment and labor assignment
   d) Large work-in-process inventories

7. ________ is by far the best among work surfaces in the kitchen.

a) Marble b) Hard wood

c) Laminated plastics d) Stainless steel

8. Equipment that is selected should be

a) Efficient b) Profitable

c) Convenient d) All the above

9. The Employees Provident Fund Act was passed in

a) 1951 b) 1952

c) 1953 d) 1954

10. BEO stands for _______.

a) Buffet Event Order b) Buffer Event Order

c) Banquet Event Order d) None of the these

11. The selection of desserts should relate the _______ of the menu.

a) Side dish b) Salads

c) Main course d) Starters

12. While roasting a food see that heat is applied to food from _______.

a) Top and bottom b) Bottom and sides

c) All sides d) None

13. The fastest dry heat method of cooking is _______.

a) Roasting b) Frying

c) Steaming d) Boiling

14. Every kitchen should provide at least ______ floor area.

a) 8-10m^2 b) 9-10 m^2

c) 10-12 m^2 d) 10-15 m^2

15. Job descriptions can be used by____________.

a) Line management b) Middle management

c) Kitchen management d) Top management

16. Which of the following is not a typical service attribute?

a) Intangible product b) Customer interaction is high

c) Easy to store d) Difficult to resell

17. ______ space is sufficient for a single person to work in the kitchen.

a) 2.5m × 3m b) 3.5m × 4m

c) 5.5m × 6m d) 6.5m × 7m

18. Service in rooms is carried out on ______.

a) By hands b) Platter or Plate

c) Trays & Trolleys d) All of these

19. The most popular style of service in banquet is ______.

a) Silver Service b) Room service

c) Preplaced d) Buffet Service

20. ______ explains the subordinate superior relationship that exists in an establishment.

a) Work chart b) Office chart

c) Organization chart d) Description chart

21. Point the correct function of management in catering operation ______.

a) Planning → organizing → coordinating → controlling → evaluating

b) Planning → controlling → organizing → coordinating → directing → controlling

c) Evaluating → planning → organizing → coordinating → directing → controlling

d) Planning → directing → evaluating → organizing → controlling → co-ordinating

22. According to Philip E. Atkinson a diary of stored data which shows the utilization of time is called as ______.

a) Data log b) Time log

c) Both d) None of these

23. Which of the following statement is/are in correct?

i) Evaluation is necessary at all times and at high levels

ii) All function of management are not closely interrelated

a) Statement (i) is true (ii) not true

b) Statement (i) is true (ii) not true

c) Both are true

d) Both are wrong

24. Who stated that principle in management is not prescriptive?
    a) Koontzo Donied b) Weibrich
    c) George d) Both a & b
25. The most accurate means of measuring ingredient is _______.
    a) Volume b) Weight
    c) Number d) Pressure
26. Which of the following is choice menu?
    a) Cyclic menu b) A la carte
    c) Table d' hote d) None of these
27. The convenience system is used mostly in _________.
    a) Hostel b) Multi-outlet food preparation
    c) Both a & b d) None of these
28. Seasoning improves _______ in food.
    a) Decreases the cooking time b) Increase the nutritive value
    c) Increase the palatability d) All
29. Which of the following food is used in finger buffet?
    a) Main dish b) Custard
    c) Finger foods d) Starters
30. The kind of motel where the formal relationship between manager and staff are flexible is _______.
    a) Hotel b) Flight catering
    c) Restaurant d) Dhaba
31. The process of decision making involves _______.
    a) Making a mental effort
    b) Listing out alterative courses of action within the structure of a situation
    c) Choosing a single course of action among many alternative
    d) All of these
32. Which of the following would not be an operations function in a fast-food restaurant?
    a) Maintaining equipment b) Purchasing ingredients
    c) Advertising and promotion d) Making hamburgers

33. The time log could be recorded at regular _____ intervals.

a) Half to 1 hour
b) Half to one and half hour
c) Half or two hour
d) Half and two and half hour

34. Using colours on walls and ceilings, which absorb light will result in use of _________

a) More electricity
b) Less electricity
c) No electricity
d) None of the above

35. The methods followed in performing tasks are_______________

a) Attitudes
b) Goals
c) Desires
d) Procedures

36. FAOP means_____________

a) Fixed and Opening Price
b) Firm at Opening
c) Firm at Opening Price
d) Firm at Old Price

37. The temperature best suited for final rinse in dish washing is_________

a) 70°C
b) 80°C
c) 50°C
d) 40°C

38. Which of the following principle is most applicable to catering establishment which are constantly handling materials heavy equipment and working with steam and other fuel?

a) Work stability
b) Initiative
c) Orderliness
d) Control

39. To get rigid direction ________activities are necessary.

a) Organizing & evaluation
b) Direction &control
c) Control
d) Evaluation

40. In which year the Industrial dispute act was introduced?

a) 1947
b) 1897
c) 1900
d) 1930

41. Thali service is ______.

a) Self service
b) Room service
c) Banquet service
d) Restaurant service

42. The principle of hierarchy refers to the chain formed by _____.

a) Staff management
b) Top management
c) Middle management
d) All of these

43. Banquet is an example of _____.

a) Open market catering
b) Welfare catering
c) Restricted market catering
d) Closed market catering

44. For an assembly-serve foodservice system, where will food most likely be purchased along the food processing continuum?

a) All along the continuum
b) Middle of continuum
c) Complete end
d) None

45. The continental breakfast includes _______.

a) Fish
b) Meat
c) Bread rolls
d) Toast with jam

46. Usually jobs are divided according to the ability of ______.

a) Employee
b) Work
c) Both a & b
d) Employer

47. Who defined quality as degree of excellence?

a) Michael brown
b) John W Buick
c) Wesley Meyer
d) George

48. Lighting that falls on the ceilings makes space______.

a) Look larger
b) Look smaller
c) Look brighter
d) None of these

49. What is the suitable operative temperature for a refrigerator?

a) -18°C
b) 1 -4°C
c) 100°C
d) 8-63°C

50. Which of the following is /are the process of food production?

a) Collecting the ingredient
b) Weight and measuring
c) Preparing the sufficient food to make them ready for cooking
d) All of these

51. Buffet service is a form of ______.

a) Vending b) Waiter service

c) Self service d) Room service

52. What is the order of organization chart?

i) Activity analysis ii) Decision analysis

iii) Relation analysis

a) i) ii) iii) b) i) iii) ii)

c) ii) iii) i) d) iii) ii) i)

53. SAP means ______.

a) Subject to Added Price b) Subject to Approved Price

c) Subject to Approval of Price d) Subject to Additional Price

54. The principle of discipline covers like to ______ which are essential for smooth functioning of establishment.

a) Punctuality

b) Courtesy

c) Adherence to rules and regulation

d) All of these

55. Who authorizes purchasing in small establishment?

a) Supervisor b) Manager

c) Management d) Subordinate

56. Which of the following statement is incorrect?

a) Meal planning does not help in accurate calculation of food costs

b) Planning ensures that food is wasted

c) Washing after peeling will retain water soluble vitamins

d) All of these

57. ________ is good tool for increasing efficiently in terms of speed as well as resource utilization.

a) Job analysis b) Job description

c) Job specification d) Work schedule

58. The nutritive content of the meat products is not affected by ______.

a) Feed

b) Time

c) Breed

d) Environmental condition in which the animals are reared

59. Continuous process taking place at all levels of management is ______.

a) Controlling b) Evaluating

c) Directing d) Planning

60. A popular breakfast roll is ______.

a) Waffers b) Oatmeal

c) Croissant d) Muesli

61. The main principle in a food service establishment is __________.

a) Need and location

b) Structure, tasks and relationship

c) Both a & b

d) None of these

62. The most common tactic followed in process-layout planning is to arrange departments or work centers so they ______.

a) Minimize the cost of skilled labor

b) Minimize the costs of material handling cleaning

c) Maximize the machine utilization

d) Maximize the man power utilization

63. For which foodservice system would food costs likely be highest?

a) Conventional b) Centralized

c) Ready-prepared d) Assembly-serve

64. The relationship between manager and other staff are flexible in ______.

a) Hotel b) Restaurant

c) Dhaba d) None of these

65. Kinds of budgets in catering establishment is ______.

a) Capital budgets b) Operating budgets

c) Both a & b d) None of these

66. The subordinate superior relationship that exists in an establishment is revealed by
   a) Work chart b) Office chart
   c) Organization chart d) None of these
67. Principles are formulated on the basis of
   a) Present happenings b) Past experiences
   c) Past gains d) Past losses
68. Which of the statements is incorrect?
   a) Principles are rigid for proof rules
   b) Principles provide a hypothesis for predicting future happenings
   c) Principles should be applied with value judgment
   d) None of these
69. Planning catering operations involves
   a) Forecasting number of customers accurately
   b) Establishing profit policy
   c) Knowing staff skills for production and service
   d) All of these
70. Process involving demarcating areas of activity and then establishing activity is called
   a) Directing b) Coordinating
   c) Organizing d) Planning
71. Cafeteria is the best known example of
   a) Self service b) Waiter service
   c) Hospital service d) None of these
72. Punctuality, courtesy, adherence to rules fall under
   a) Principle of orderliness b) Principle of loyalty
   c) Principle of discipline d) Principle of unitary direction
73. The control process
   a) Measures actual performance
   b) Compare results with standards expected
   c) Pinpoint areas of deviation
   d) All of the above

74. To give rigid direction to activities, ____ is necessary

a) Evaluation b) Organizing

c) Control d) Direction

75. Standards for placement of staff in higher positions for which they are found to have skills is provided by

a) Planning b) Organizing

c) Control d) Evaluation

76. Appraisal of work conditions and procedures involves

a) Evaluating structures, plans, jobs

b) Degree of lighting and ventilation

c) Analyzing ergonomic aspects

d) All of these

77. Food products can be evaluated using

a) Rating scales

b) Score sheets

c) Both a and b

d) Visually

78. The methods that make use of instruments to measure quality of food are

a) Sensory methods b) Objective methods

c) Chemical methods d) Physical methods

79. The nutritional quality of the food can be judged through

a) Sensory evaluation b) Chemical evaluation

c) Objective evaluation d) Physical evaluation

80. Choose the correct series of steps in organizing

i) Resource allocation

ii) Equal distribution of work load

iii) Activity is broken down into specification units

iv) Allocating staff

v) Allocating each unit to a management group

a) v, iv, iii, ii, i b) iv, iii, ii, i, v

c) iii, ii, i, v, iv d) iii, v, iv, i, ii

81. The function that initiates actual performance of tasks and requires greater interaction between people is

a) Organizing b) Coordinating
c) Directing d) Evaluating

82. The maximum time to be spent for planning by a catering manager will be

a) 50% b) 40%
c) 30% d) 20%

83. "Keeping a watch" on what is going on is

a) Guiding b) Supervising
c) Instructing d) Teaching

84. Which of the following statement is incorrect?

a) Good supervision helps in maximizing resource use
b) There are only few ways in which supervision can be carried out effectively
c) Supervision is possible through a regular round or activity areas or work centers
d) Directing or leading people depends greatly on the personality of the manager

85. The binding together, unifying and harmonizing of all activities and efforts is considered as ____________

a) Unification b) Coordination
c) Diversification d) Dissemination

86. Which of the statements is incorrect?

a) Management is an exercise in coordination
b) All functions of management needs to be coordinated to achieve goals
c) Coordination is not that important in individual efforts
d) Coordination is necessary if group efforts are to become meaningful

87. If the food costs are too high, it can be indicative of

a) Pilferage of food from stock
b) Prices too high
c) Excessive wastage in preparation
d) All of the above

88. What is the order of functions of management?

1. Directing 2. Controlling

3. Organizing 4. Evaluating

5. Planning

a) 5,4,3,2,1 b) 4,3,2,1,5

c) 3,2,1,5,4 d) 5,3,1,2,4

89. Authority and responsibility passes on in ________________

a) Line relationship b) Line-staff relationship

c) Staff-line relationship d) None of these

90. The expertise of staff utilized to maximize the efficiency of line personnel to the utmost is

a) Line relationship b) Line-staff relationship

c) Staff-line relationship d) None of the above

91. The relationship between manager and other staff are flexible in

a) Dhaba b) Restaurant

c) Flight catering d) Ship catering

92. The effective tool for managing at entry level of the organization structure is

a) Job specification b) Job description

c) Work schedule d) Work simplification

93. Caustic soda, soda ash, sodium gluconate are

a) Detergents b) Sterilants

c) Abrasives d) Corrosives

94. Job analysis sheets can be used by

a) Middle management b) Kitchen management

c) Line management d) Top management

95. Plans for staffing and menus, price lists can be used by

a) Middle management b) Kitchen management

c) Line management d) Top management

96. Plans for sales, purchase, recruitment can be used by

a) Middle management b) Kitchen management

c) Line management d) Top management

97. A statement indicating standards to be achieved for a particular job is called

a) Job description   b) Job specification

c) Work schedule   d) Work flow

98. Small establishments may use _______ instead _________ because clear supervision is possible at work.

a) Job description, job specification

b) Job specification, job description

c) Work schedule, job description

d) Job specification, work schedule

99. Outline of the work or job to be done by an employee is called as

a) Job description   b) Job specification

c) Work schedule   d) Job analysis sheet

100. Job analysis is also sometimes referred to as

a) Work analysis   b) Job specification

c) Job description   d) Task analysis

101. Which of the following is a very good tool for increasing efficiently both in terms of speed as well as resource utilization?

a) Job specification   b) Job description

c) Job analysis   d) Work schedule

102. Which of the following is the projected plan for the operation of a business?

a) Work schedule

b) Task analysis

c) Budget

d) Production and service analysis statements

103. Cash budget comes under

a) Capital budget   b) Operating budget

c) Both a and b   d) Sales budget

104. Sales budget, labour, cost budget and maintenance comes under

a) Capital budget   b) Operating budget

c) Both a and b   d) None of these

105. Budgets help to determine the

a) Proportion of variable and semi variable costs

b) Cash position of the establishment

c) Amount of expenditure

d) All of these

106. The influential increment over and above mechanical compliance with the routine directives of the organization is known as

a) Workmanship b) Leadership

c) Management d) Participation

107. Identify the correct series in decision making

1. Listing out alternative courses of action

2. Making a mental effort

3. Choosing from among many alternatives, a single course of action

a) 1,2,3 b) 3,2,1

c) 2,1,3 d) 2,3,1

108. The ability of people to evaluate accuratelyany situation or message is known as

a) Hello effect b) Halo effect

c) Cello effect d) Helo effect

109. The ability of an individual to interact in a group and establish smooth flow of communication is the index of

a) Peripherality b) Centrality

c) Congeniality d) Multiplexity

110. If the index of _____ is higher, the level of interaction is lower

a) Peripherality b) Centrality

c) Congeniality d) Multiplexity

111. The ability to convey information or messages to others so that they can understand and interpret them in the same light as the sender of the message is known as

a) Interpretation b) Communication

c) Dissemination d) Popularization

112. The index of __________ is higher, if the liaison quality of that position is higher.

a) Peripherality b) Congeniality

c) Centrality d) Multiplexity

113. Any form of communication is complete, only if there is a ________ from the receptor(s).

a) Action b) Feedback

c) Positive reaction d) Negative reaction

114. Hard water used for dish washing

a) Neither reduces nor increases b) medium boiler efficiency

c) Increases boiler efficiency d) Reduce boiler efficiency

115. Good pay will

a) Increase labour turnover b) Reduce labour turnover

c) Balance labour turnover d) None of these

116. Clear-cut goals and work schedules will

a) Minimize utility of time b) Maximize utility of time

c) Balance utility of time d) None of these

117. Socializing at work in kitchen and service areas will lead to

a) Work simplification b) Time wasting

c) Work easily done d) None of these

118. Using colors on walls and ceilings, which absorb light will result in use of

a) More electricity b) Less electricity

c) No electricity d) None of these

119. The methods followed in performing tasks are referred to as

a) Attitudes b) Goals

c) Desires d) Procedures

120. The most common shape in kitchen is

a) Rectangular kitchen b) U-shaped kitchen

c) L-shaped kitchen d) Parallel kitchen

121. The kitchen that is step-saving is

a) L-shaped kitchen b) U-shaped kitchen

c) Parallel kitchen d) Straight line kitchen

122. Most efficient design where floor space is limited is

a) Parallel kitchen b) U-shaped kitchen
c) L-shaped kitchen d) Square kitchen

123. Best suited kitchen for cafeterias of the self service type is

a) L-shaped kitchen b) Parallel kitchen
c) U-shaped kitchen d) None of these

124. Useful arrangement for kiosks, tea shops or mobile vending units is

a) L-shaped kitchen b) U-shaped kitchen
c) Straight line kitchen d) Parallel kitchen

125. The average recommended height for work surfaces is

a) 200 cms b) 150 cms
c) 100 cms d) 90 cms

126. Organization structures can grow in ____________

a) Parallel b) Horizontal
c) Diagonal d) All the above

127. An organization chart with three types of analysis was developed by ____________

a) George b) Drucker
c) Michelles d) James

128. Tools of management have been developed by

a) Decision makers b) Supervisors
c) Managers d) Law line staff

129. The method of serving meals to customers in trains and aircraft is

a) Banquet service b) Buffet service
c) Cafeteria self service d) Vending service

130. Gourmet foods means

a) Prepared fresh products
b) Food decorations
c) Specialty and imported food products
d) Preserved foods

131. Linen, disposable mats, plates, cups etc are stores in

a) Equipment store b) Trash store

c) Store for cleaning supplies d) Miscellaneous storage

132. The temperature for refrigerated storage is

a) 0-10ºC b) 0-5ºC

c) 0-20ºC d) -20ºC

133. Dairy products must be stored at a temperature of

a) 1.1ºC to 7.2ºC b) 3.3ºC to 7.8ºC

c) 0.6ºC to 3.3ºC d) -5ºC to -1.1ºC

134. Windows and exhaust fans should be situated

a) High up on the walls b) At medium height on the walls

c) At shoulder level on the walls d) None of these

135. The temperature for cold storage is

a) 5-10ºC b) 0-5ºC

c) 10-15ºC d) 15-20ºC

136. The light omitted when a substance is heated is

a) Combustion b) Electric discharge

c) Incandescence d) Fluorescence

137. The purchase where the buyer does not hold the stock of the items , and supplier who are nearest to the location of the establishment is

a) Auction buying b) Consignment buying

c) Negotiated buying d) Blanket order purchasing

138. FSQS means

a) Food Safety and Quantity Service

b) Food Standard and Quantity Service

c) Food Safety and Quality Service

d) Food Standard and Quality Service

139. Food service outlets best suited for the provision of ready to eat snacks and beverages to the public are

a) Restaurants b) Dhabas

c) Kiosks d) Motels

140. Every food buyer needs to posses

a) High moral and ethical values b) Loyalty to the institution

c) Loyalty to customers d) All of these above qualities

141. If buyer agrees to take the supplies at a price established in the future, the contract is said to be

a) SAP b) FAOP

c) Whole sale buying d) Retail buying

142. If the buyer has the option of rejecting the order if the price fixed in the future is not acceptable to him, then the contract is said to be

a) SAP b) FAOP

c) Whole sale buying d) Retail buying

143. The purpose of seasoning is to _________of food.

a) Increase colour of food b) Decrease the cooking time

c) Increase the nutritive value d) Increase the palatability

144. KOT is ____________

a) Kitchen Operation Ticket b) Kitchen Operation Token

c) Kitchen Order Token d) Kitchen Order Ticket

145. In planning a menu, what should be considered?

a) Habits of the customer

b) Purchasing power/ favourites of the customer

c) Satiety value and value for money

d) All of these

146. A choice menu offering choices of dishes to customers is

a) Table d'hôte menu b) A la carte menu

c) A combination of both d) None of these

147. A set menu in which a number of dishes are planned and offered a set price is

a) A la carte menu b) Table d'hôte menu

c) A combination of both d) None of these

148. Which of the following statements is incorrect?

a) A la carte menu are hardly ever changed

b) Table d'hôte menu are changed more frequently

c) It is advisable to change menu plans frequently

d) Table d'hôte menus change with the same price range

149. Menu planning is an art involving

a) Knowledge, thought b) Insight

c) Creativity and initiative d) All of these

150. Braising is a _________ cooking method

a) Moist heat b) Dry heat

c) Combination method d) Microwaving

151. The light omitted when a substance is heated

a) Combustion b) Incandescence

c) Negotiated buying d) Blanket order purchasing

152. In American service food is served _______ side.

a) Right b) Left

c) Centre d) None

153. Serving of food in the Asian type is called _______.

a) Buffet b) Banquet

c) Restaurant d) Vending

154. Which of the following is not hindering force?

a) Rising price and structural damage

b) Rising price and food shortage

c) Cordial staff relations and good management

d) All of these

155. The average recommended height for work surfaces is

a) 100 cm b) 90 cm

c) 150 cm d) 200 cm

156. In general guide _______ is suitable for a double person to work in kitchen.

a) 2.5m ×4m b) 2m ×4m

c) 2m ×3m d) 2.5 ×3m

157. In formal menu, the maximum number of courses is

a) 4 b) 5

c) 6 d) 7

158. Factors affecting turnover of the customer is ______
   a) Choice of food
   b) The Time at for Customer Disposal
   c) The Method of Service
   d) All of These
159. The principle which is related to co-ordination of activities to achieve a single goal is ______
   a) Unitary direction b) Unitary command
   c) Orderliness d) Work stability
160. Why payment or remuneration is important to workers ______.
   a) To do their best b) To motivate
   c) To satisfy d) All of these
161. While planning and organizing requires mental effort on the part of the management is done by ______
   a) Instructing b) Guiding
   c) Supervising d) All of these
162. The forces which give achievement in food service establishment is ______
   a) Helping force b) Hindering force
   c) Both a & b d) None of these
163. ______ enhances the structural beauty and color of walls, ceilings, floor, furnishing
   a) Illumination b) Artificial light
   c) Solar light d) None of these
164. Illumination is measured in units called ______
   a) Lux b) Luz
   c) Lus d) Luze
165. The light emitted by unit area of surface is commonly measured in ______.
   a) Candelas per square meter b) Candelux per square
   c) Candelax per square meter d) Candelas per square
166. The recommended illumination levels for coffee shop is ______
   a) 150 lux b) 200 lux
   c) 250 lux d) 300 lux

167. The illumination levels for dining room, grills, restaurant and cafeterias is ________.

a) 50 lux b) 100 lux

c) 150 lux d) 200 lux

168. The illumination level for food production areas is ________.

a) 300 lux b) 400 lux

c) 500 lux d) 450 lux

169. ________ is the place where one can eat and pay for the same.

a) Restaurant b) Pubs

c) Spa d) All

170. Common size of the modular trays is ________.

a) 130 × 40 cm b) 32 × 40cm

c) 30×42cm d) 31×45cm

171. Quality of water for dish washing means ________.

a) Polluted and soft b) Unpolluted and soft

c) Polluted and hard d) Unpolluted and hard

172. Which is the best method to cook vegetables?

a) Frying b) Steaming

c) Baking d) All

173. Which of the following is best option for home saving?

a) Bank b) Post office

c) Both a & b d) Chits

174. A good layout requires determining ________.

a) Environment and aesthetics

b) Capacity and space requirements

c) Material handling requirements

d) All

175. A food service establishment before making profit should invest on ________.

a) Money b) Labour

c) Utensils d) Area

176. A detergent cannot function as ________.

a) Stain removing agent b) Cleansing agent

c) Sterilizing agent d) Bleaching agent

177. Sugars, flour, cereals are stored in ______.

a) Jute bags b) Cases

c) Tins d) Jars

178. Open drains are a health hazards as they ______.

a) Are breeding place for mosquitoes

b) Emit foul smell

c) Look ugly

d) Do not let the water flow easily

179. The menu shouldn't overshoot the ______.

a) Budget b) Overhead cost

c) Semi-variable cost d) None

180. The liquid from cooked meat or vegetable are ______.

a) Consomme b) Broth

c) Disques d) Stock

181. The accurate means of measure are needed for ______.

a) Portioning foods for service

b) Receiving and issuing supplies

c) Measuring ingredients for formulas

d) All the above

182. The smoking point of frying medium when fresh should not be less than ______.

a) 100°C b) 120°C

c) 200°C d) 20°C

183. How many courses are available in the banquet menu?

a) Two courses b) Three courses

c) More than four d) None

184. The most important resources for any establishment today is ______.

a) Management skill

b) Management security

c) Customer relationship with management

d) All

185. As the length of the structure increases coordinating the activities of the establishment becomes ________.

a) Constant b) Difficult

c) Easy d) None of these

186. The second name of Russian service is ______.

a) American service b) English service

c) European service d) Compromise service

187. Incandescent bubbles give a ______ light as compared to fluorescent light.

a) Warm b) Cold

c) Bright d) All

188. The other name of apartment service is ______.

a) Buffet service b) Compromise service

c) Blue-plate service d) None

189. The average serving of beef with bone is ______.

a) 3.5 oz b) 2.8 oz

c) 1.6 oz d) 4.5 oz

190. In a cyclic menu, the menus are repeated on a ________ basis.

a) Weekly b) Weekly or monthly

c) Monthly d) Yearly

191. Soft water means ______.

a) Rain water b) Not foaming with soap

c) Foaming with soap d) None of these

192. The process of introducing new corner to environment is ______.

a) Insulation b) Induction

c) Installation d) Conduction

193. Budgets help to determine ______.

a) Amount of expenditure
b) Cash position
c) Proportion of variables
d) All of these

194. The influential increment over and above mechanical compliance with routine directives of the organization is known as ______.

a) Management
b) Participation
c) Leadership
d) Workmanship

195. Organoleptic evaluation of the food can be judged through ______.

a) Physical evaluation
b) Chemical evaluation
c) Sensory evaluation
d) Objective evaluation

196. Causes of staff turnover in catering establishment ______.

a) Unsociable shift
b) Barring pay packet
c) Union
d) All of these

197. The control process is ______.

a) Measure actual performance
b) Comparing result with present situation
c) Pinpoint deviation
d) All of these

198. Which of the following is not a typical attribute of goods?

a) Output can be resold
b) Production and consumption are separate
c) Often easy to automate
d) Aspects of quality difficult to measure

199. The usefulness of many small piece of equipments are influenced by ______.

a) Design
b) Size
c) Material and sturdiness
d) All of these

200. According to peter Michal the policy of multi skilling staff instead of making them specialist increases their______.

a) Performance
b) Confusion
c) Immoral
d) Creativity

201. Selection of equipment is directly affected by the ______.
   a) The volume of food prepared b) Types of food prepared
   c) Both d) None of these
202. Which of the following measure can be taken to reduce labour turnover?
   a) Good pay
   b) Favourable conditions of work
   c) Taking care of people through employee welfare scheme
   d) All the above
203. Which of the following inputs has the greatest potential to increase productivity?
   a) Labor b) Capital
   c) Management d) None of these
204. The objective of food preparation is ______.
   a) Assurance of safety for human consumption
   b) Improvement of digestibility
   c) Conservation of the nutritive value of the food
   d) All the above
205. The size of the quarter plate is ______.
   a) 3.25 x 4.25 inches b) 4.25 x 5.5 inches
   c) 6.5 x 8.5 inches d) 16.5 x 21.5 cm
206. The size of a soup cup is _______.
   a) 9 oz to 12 oz b) 6oz to 8oz
   c) 8 oz to 10 oz d) 10 oz to 12 oz
207. Size and shape of the space in kitchen is directly related to ______.
   a) Type of equipment b) Size of equipment
   c) Both a and b d) Number of equipment
208. Semi fixed cost is also known as ________.
   a) Fixed costs b) Semi variable cost
   c) Variable cost d) None of these
209. ____ cost which can't be directly identified with food products.
   a) Cost of materials b) cost of employees
   c) Overhead cost d) None of these

210. Equipment selection depends on ________.

a) Pre-preparation b) Method of preparation

c) Amount to be cooked d) All the above

211. In ________ service hot food is placed in bain-marie in full view of the customer.

a) Plated service b) Tray service

c) Fork buffet d) Full buffet

212. Which of following is/are cost involved in catering?

a) Food costs b) Labour costs

c) Overhead cost d) All of these

213. At the temperature of a refrigerator most food poisoning bacteria are ______.

a) Inactive b) Form spores

c) Multiply hastily d) Die

214. ______ is a self-service.

a) Russian service b) Gueridon service

c) Buffet service d) Room service

215. Removal of permanent hardness of water is done by ________.

a) By boiling b) By adding caustic soda

c) Calgon process d) Clark's process

216. Mobile catering offer meals at _____ prices to customers.

a) Costlier b) Fixed

c) Lower d) None

217. Which of the following is not a common type of fire extinguisher?

a) Water Based b) CO_2 based

c) Foam Based d) Hydrogen Based

218. Food served "straight from the fire" is _______.

a) Plated servicue b) Trayed service

c) Waiter service d) Buffet service

219. Which of following statement is correct?
   a) Cutting vegetables on a chopping board with a sharp knife makes chopping of small quantities easier
   b) Kneading machine for dough preparation is handy, not safe and quick
   c) Using power equipment keep us work simplification
   d) Changing one variable results in a time reduction of 40 and 60 percent respectively

220. Due to _____ the choice is generally limited in mobile catering.
   a) Lack of equipments   b) Lack of space
   c) Lack of labours   d) Lack of money

221. The number of waiters involved in buffet service is ______.
   a) 2-4   b) 4-6
   c) 6-8   d) 8-10

222. Which of the statement is correct?
   a) Salads, desserts should not held in freezing
   b) Soups, curries should not held in preheated bain-marie
   c) Ice cream not be held at -3^{0}c
   d) None of these

223. Which of the following decisions have to be implemented before establishing catering institutions?
   a) Control system
   b) Suitability
   c) Area of space within the building
   d) All of these

224. Food product can be evaluated using _______.
   a) Rating scales   b) Score sheets
   c) None of these   d) Both a and b

225. Selection of desserts should relate the ________ of the menu.
   a) Side dish   b) Salads
   c) Starters   d) Main course

226. Which of the following household equipment is a time and energy saving device?

a) Television b) Telephone
c) DVD player d) Pressure cooker

227. The main reason for keeping kitchen clean is _______.

a) To slowdown bacterial growth
b) To reduce the chance of bacteria finding food
c) To give a good impression to customers
d) To prevent contamination of food

228. In ______ service customers are required to come to a counter, bay or table to serve themselves.

a) Buffet service b) Self service
c) Banquet service d) Room service

229. The substance used in the preparation of foods to enhance their natural flavor is called as______________.

a) Shortening agents b) Leavening agents
c) Food adjuncts d) None of these

230. Which of the following is formal service?

a) Self service b) Room service
c) Banquet service d) restaurant service

231. Which of the following are used for placing advance breakfast orders?

a) Clean my Room card b) Menu card kept in rooms
c) Room Service door knob Card d) None

232. Personal hygiene refers to the _____.

a) Personal grooming
b) General health
c) Working habits of the all people who are working in an establishment
d) All

233. In _____ service meals are served to customers in transit, as on trains and aircraft.

a) Plated b) Buffet
c) Tray d) Banquet

234. Finger foods are available in _____ buffet.

a) Full buffet
b) Finger buffet
c) Fork buffet
d) Tray service

235. Buffets are classified into _____ types according to the menus planned.

a) 6
b) 4
c) 2
d) 3

236. Tools of management have been developed by _______.

a) Decision making
b) Managers
c) Managing directors
d) None of these

237. Organization structure can grow in _________ direction.

a) Horizontal
b) Parallel
c) Diagonal
d) None of these

238. The use of ________ during cooking destroys trace elements.

a) Sodium chloride
b) Sodium bicarbonate
c) Lemon juice
d) None of these

239. The traditional wayside eating place is known as _______.

a) Motel
b) Hotel
c) Dhaba
d) Restaurant

240. The India Tourism Development Corporation started a regular mobile lunch service for __________.

a) Office goers
b) School students
c) Poor people
d) Orphans

241. Silver sand is an example of __________.

a) Corrosives
b) Abrasives
c) Sterilizers
d) Detergents

242. Maintaining a diary or a time log to manage time was suggested by __________.

a) Dereck
b) Michael
c) Philip
d) Anderson

243. An ancient method of serving food is _______________.

a) Buffet
b) Banquet
c) Vending
d) Restaurant

244. The peak period for service in a food service institution is ______.

a) 11-11.30 pm b) 12.30- 1.30 pm

c) 12.30- 2 pm d) 12.30-3.30 pm

245. A preserved combination of two or more fruits with nuts and raisins is called ______.

a) Conserve b) Jam

c) Marmalade d) Pickle

246. Caustic soda and Soda ash are present in______.

a) Corrosives b) Abrasives

c) Sterilizers d) Detergents

247. In the place where the nutritious and satisfying snacks served are ______.

a) Industrial employee canteen b) College or school canteen

c) Office canteen d) Public canteen

248. Which of the following is not a type of storage?

a) Hot storage b) Refrigerator storage

c) Low temperature storage d) Room temperature storage

249. According to Drucker, an organization chart is charted out by ______ types of analysis.

a) Five b) Two

c) Three d) Six

250. The main principle in a food service establishment is______

a) Need and location b) Structure, tasks and relationship

c) Motivation and choice d) All the above

Answers

1. b 2. a 3. d 4. a 5. d 6. c 7. d 8. d 9. b 10. c

11. c 12. c 13. a 14. b 15. c 16. c 17. a 18. c 19. d 20. c

21. a 22. c 23. d 24. d 25. b 26. b 27. c 28. c 29. c 30. d

31. d 32. c 33. a 34. a 35. d 36. b 37. b 38. c 39. c 40. b

41. d 42. d 43. c 44. c 45. c 46. d 47. b 48. b 49. d 50. d

51. c 52. a 53. c 54. d 55. b 56. d 57. a 58. d 59. d 60. c

61. c 62. b 63. d 64. c 65. c 66. c 67. b 68. a 69. d 70. c

71. a 72. c 73. d 74. c 75. d 76. d 77. c 78. b 79. b 80. d

81. c 82. d 83. b 84. b 85. b 86. d 87. d 88. d 89. a 90. b

91. a 92. b 93. a 94. b 95. a 96. d 97. b 98. a 99. c 100. d

101. c 102. c 103. a 104. b 105. d 106. b 107. c 108. b 109. b 110. a

111. b 112. c 113. b 114. d 115. b 116. b 117. b 118. a 119. d 120. a

121. b 122. c 123. b 124. c 125. d 126. b 127. c 128. c 129. a 130. c

131. d 132. a 133. b 134. a 135. b 136. c 137. b 138. c 139. c 140. d

141. b 142. a 143. d 144. d 145. d 146. b 147. b 148. c 149. d 150. c

151. b 152. a 153. d 154. c 155. b 156. a 157. a 158. d 159. a 160. d

161. d 162. c 63. b 164. a 165. a 166. a 167. b 168. c 169. a 170. a

171. b 172. b 173. c 174. d 175. a 176. c 177. a 178. a 179. a 180. b

181. d 182. d 183. c 184. a 185. b 186. c 187. a 188. c 189. a 190. b

191. c 192. b 193. d 194. c 195. c 196. d 197. d 198. d 199. d 200. a

201. a 202. d 203. c 204. d 205. a 206. b 207. c 208. b 209. c 210. a

211. a 212. d 213. a 214. c 215. b 216. d 217. c 218. d 219. a 220. c

221. b 222. c 223. a 224. d 225. d 226. a 227. d 228. d 229. b 230. c

231. c 232. c 233. d 234. c 235. b 236. d 237. b 238. a 239. b 240. c

241. a 242. b 243. c 244. d 245. b 246. a 247. d 248. b 249. a 250. d

7

Extension Education and Communication

1. "Extension Education is formal and informal education" Who said this?

   a) O.P. Dahama b) L.D. Kalsey
   c) M.C. Burret d) D. Ensoninger

2. Who said that, we can define Extension Education as the increased dissemination of useful knowledge for improving rural life?

   a) D. Ensminger b) O.P. Dahama
   c) H.W. Butt d) B. Rambhai

3. Who stated about curriculum 'is the price of employment of models is eternal vigilance'?

   a) Fred Clarks b) Rousseau
   c) Durkheim d) None

4. A diagrammatic representation of numerical or qualitative data

   a) Graph b) Photograph
   c) Diagram d) None

5. The liquidation of mass illiteracy is necessary not only for promoting participation in the working of democratic institutions but for ________ specially for farmers

   a) Education b) Finance
   c) Production d) None

6. In informal education there is no

   a) Curriculum, fees strechive, examination and formal teaching
   b) Formal teaching and curriculum
   c) Curriculum and fee strechive
   d) Curriculum, examination and fee strechive

7. Lack of coordination brings about
   a) Conflict, friction b) Overlapping
   c) Duplications d) All of these
8. Organization in administration is
   a) Arrangement of material b) Arrangement of individual
   c) Both a and b d) Only a
9. What does it indicate in administration "that affects the decision, gives the signal to act indicates what action is to be and when it is to start and stop. It is the authority on the move"
   a) Organization b) Direction
   c) Coordination d) None
10. The visual aids shown to the participants should be of __________ size so that those sitting at the back can see it
    a) 20X10" b) 15X9"
    c) 10X8" d) None
11. Self employed women association is made by ______.
    a) Ela shatt b) Rolling
    c) Engel crew d) Swansous
12. The secondary education commission has referred to indiscipline namely
    a) Individual and non aggressive b) Individual and collective
    c) Collective and aggressive d) Aggressive and non aggressive
13. Professional discussions rarely go beyond
    a) Phatic stage b) Personal stage
    c) Intimate stage d) None
14. Robert shuter states "In this stage communications reveal their innermost thoughts and feeling- their fear and joys, weakness and strengths. This stage is
    a) Phatic stage b) Personal stage
    c) Intimate state d) None
15. ____ programme are not succeed in absence of whole family members.
    a) Girl education programme b) Adult education programme
    c) Skill development programme d) All of these

16. The process of conversion of the subject matter into symbols is called as

a) Encoding b) Decoding

c) Channel d) None

17. Who stated that "communication is a process of people interacting through use of message?

a) Zeuschner b) Skinner

c) Rama Krishna d) Sagar

18. Communication is the art of

a) Speaking and gestures b) Appearance and impact

c) Persuasion and motivation d) None

19. Communication is a primary tool for effective

a) Speaking b) Behaviour change

c) Impact d) None

20. A connotation meaning is the relationship between a

a) Snig b) Object

c) Person d) All

21. Which of the following is not an objective of extension education?

a) Social-cultural –development of the community

b) Education –change the outlook of people

c) Material –increases production income

d) Non-social – encourage related activities

22. Why is it so important to quote people in order to understand what someone means

a) Denotative meaning b) Connotative meaning

c) Contextual meaning d) Structural meaning

23. The type of receiver influences the communicator's decisions regarding

a) Message content, tone, channel, timing

b) Tone and channel

c) Message content, channel and timing

d) Channel and timing

24. Feedback enables the communicator to carry out

a) Corrections b) Amendments

c) Change message d) All

25. Branch of the home science extension are ______.
   a) Child development b) Food science
   c) Textile and Clothing d) All of these
26. Usually _____ mm film is used for educational purpose in motion picture.
   a) 70 b) 35
   c) 16 d) 20
27. _______ is concerned with the educational growth of children and youth preparing for life.
   a) Extension teacher b) Class room teacher
   c) Both a & b d) None
28. The system in a language providing for the orderly presentation of words is called
   a) Grammar sequence b) Syntax
   c) Comprehension d) None
29. Ordinary art appeal to man's intellect and fine art appeal to his
   a) Intellect and emotions b) Behaviour and emotions
   c) Voice and emotions d) Intellect and behaviour
30. The familiar format and content of folk media as the ______ make for clarity in communication.
   a) Duration b) Frequency
   c) Colloquial dialects d) Repetition
31. Studies show that folk traditions are uniformly popular regardless of the _____ standing of any community
   a) Education b) Social
   c) Financial d) Any
32. Puppetry becomes a valuable _____ only if the message to be communicated is developed in dramatic terms.
   a) Art b) Visual aid
   c) Guzzet d) None
33. Puppet historians tell us that nearly _________ years ago in ancient India the only form of theatre was the puppet theatre.
   a) 2000 b) 1500
   c) 1000 d) 500

34. One study estimates the existence of about 7000 street theatre group in different parts of the country with the largest number in

a) West Bengal b) Andhra

c) Tamil Nadu d) Kerala

35. Who stated "If science is poorly taught and badly learnt, it is little more than burdening the mind with dead information, and it could degenerate even into a new superstition.

a) Rousseau b) Kothari commission report

c) Froeble d) Montessori

36. Lecture demonstration method can be said to achieve

a) Insight b) Conditioning

c) Concrete to abstract d) None

37. Assignment should suit ____________of the students

a) Age b) Abilities

c) Intelligence d) All

38. In a country like India the problem and difficulty faced in assignment method is/are

a) Distance b) Well-equipped library

c) Conveyance d) Time

39. In audio-visual aid teaching students can

a) Discuss b) Question

c) Comment d) All

40. The most cheap and convenient material to use with flannel is

a) Blotting paper b) Carbon paper

c) A-4 paper d) None

41. Bulletin board provides opportunity for developing

a) Creativeness b) Responsibility

c) Knowledge d) All

42. The existence of electromagnetic waves was predicted by Maxwell in

a) 1850 b) 1865

c) 1855 d) 1875

43. ______ is accident type of education learning which happen by chance at home place or work or travel.
a) Formal education b) Informal education
c) Both d) None
44. Who developed extension education in community development?
a) Sagar b) Rama krishana
c) Skinner d) Leagans
45. An Italian Engineer was the first to demonstrate the actual transmission and reception of message. He was
a) G. Marconi b) Hartoz
c) Maxwell d) None
46. Who stated " Radio is not an addition to education. Radio is not something to be placed on top of education. Rather, radio is education."
a) Reynolds R.G b) George Watson
c) F. Wittis d) None
47. A person spends about ________ of his active time communicating
a) 20-30% b) 30-40%
c) 45-50% d) 50-60%
48. In oral communication ____________ of information will be lost.
a) 30% b) 40%
c) 20% d) 10%
49. "Tunnel Vision" with regard to communication is referred to the emotion of
a) Love b) Hate
c) Fear d) None
50. Jargon language which is special to technology, law, commerce, etc, when used can cause
a) Isolation b) Alertness
c) Emotional reaction d) Limited communication
51. The groups which are taken into account for communication is/are
a) Cultural groups and social groups
b) Family groups
c) Reference group
d) All

52. "The complex of values, ideas, attitudes, and other meaningful symbols created by man to shape human behaviour and the artifacts of that behaviour as they are transmitted from one generation to the next"

a) Culture b) Civilization

c) Adaption d) None

53. For what reason communication happen?

a) To establish or maintain interpersonal relationships

b) To acquire different kinds of knowledge

c) To help people

d) All

54. Which are the components of communication process?

a) Message, Noise, Feedback

b) Message, Recording, Feedback

c) Feedback, Message, Critiquing

d) Sender, Channel, Receiver

55. Interpersonal communication occurs only when _______.

a) An individual converses with people they have no interest in knowing

b) Three or more people are communicating with each other at the same time

c) An individual interacts with another person as a unique individual

d) Intimate conversation takes place

56. Two or more persons in reciprocal communication and interaction is called a

a) Social group b) Psychological group

c) Physical group d) Family group

57. Which of the following is dependent on what the audience does in response to message in communication?

a) Attention b) Pay on

c) Pay off d) Listing

58. The role of co-ordination in a satellite programme is

a) Crucial b) Difficult

c) Time consuming d) Expensive

59. Radio experiments in the use of radio for promoting literacy and education was conducted as early as

a) 1900s b) 1920s
c) 1930s d) 1940s

60. Display serves important purposes such as

a) Stimulating students b) Help explain thing
c) Publicize abstract ideas d) Give recognition to students work

61. According to Lee Thayer, the function of communication is given as four I's are ______.

a) Implementation, Information, Influence, Instructive
b) Information, Influence, Instructive, Integration
c) Interest, Implementation, Influence, Instructive
d) Involvement, Integration, Instruction, influence

62. In ________ there are resident welfare associations whose elected member acts as local leader.

a) Rural areas b) Urban areas
c) Both a & b d) None

63. LCD and OHP are the communication of ________.

a) Interpersonal channel b) Mass media
c) Both d) None

64. Huddle system are termed as ________.

a) Buzz session b) Forum
c) Debate d) None

65. The objective of the rural development programme is to develop ______.

a) People-people leadership b) People's participation
c) People organization d) People administration

66. According to the view of Karl Marx education aims at producing

a) Employed person b) Business man
c) Fully developed d) None

67. ________ refers to a set of verbal non verbal or written symbols arranged in a particular order that has a particular meaning to communication and the receiver.

a) Channel b) Communication
c) Content d) Code

68. Which of the country succeeds in eradication illiteracy in < 20 years

a) Pakistan b) India
c) Russia d) USA

69. Charts try to explain

a) How of events b) Express a product
c) Symbolize matter d) All

70. The below listed are some types of interpersonal skills needed in an organizational environment ______

a) Verbal and Non verbal
b) Problem solving and decision making
c) Negotiation and assertiveness
d) All of the above

71. Plywood can be used for ________.

a) Rigid chalk board b) Fiber board
c) Leather board d) None

72. National extension service was established in _______.

a) 1952 b) 1953
c) 1949 d) 1945

73. An extension worker has to bring about changes in ______.

a) Value b) Beliefs
c) Attitudes d) All of these

74. Sometimes advertisements can ______.

a) Cool us b) Rule us
c) Fool us d) All of these

75. Day dreaming is a ______.

a) Physical barrier b) Psychological barrier
c) Cultural barrier d) Semantic barrier

76. ______ is the response from the receiver to the source of the message.

a) Face to face conversation
b) Cultural model
c) Power-in-communication model
d) Feedback

77. Which is not a projective technique?

a) Model b) Flash card

c) Slides d) Photograph

78. In modern times there is increase in ______.

a) Nuclear family b) Joint family

c) Both a and b d) None

79. Interpersonal communication helps one ______.

a) To become a talented public speaker

b) Communicate with the general public

c) Learn about oneself

d) To know what others are thinking

80. Test that has been used in certain situations as part of basis for selection of professional leaders are ______.

a) Battery of test b) Cedderless group test

c) Performance test d) Achievement test

81. The media is the powerful tool for changing people's ________

a) Perceptions b) Attitudes

c) Aspirations d) All

82. Any idea, practice or product which an individual perceives to be new is ________.

a) Adoption b) Different

c) Innovation d) None

83. The degree to which an innovation is perceived as better than existing idea or object is termed as

a) Trial b) Relative advantage

c) Adoption d) None

84. The degree to which an innovation perceives to fit into a person's ways of doing things is__________.

a) Compatibility b) Comfortable

c) Adoption d) None

85. The adoption of acupuncture by American physician has been slow because

a) Not compatible with belief b) No anethelying

c) Less meaningful d) All

86. The more compatible an innovation is with a person's ______ the more rapid its rate of adoption

a) Need structure b) Values and beliefs

c) Past experiences d) All

87. The degree to which the result of an innovation are visible to others

a) Observability b) Communicability

c) Complexity d) Both a & b

88. Ways to reduce dissonance include

a) Seek additional information

b) Rationalize the situation

c) Eliminate or alter some elements

d) All of the above

89. The time which elapses between a person's initial awareness of an innovation and his decision to adopt or reject the innovation is ________.

a) Time frame b) Time interval

c) Innovation decision period d) None

90. The final group to adopt an innovation. These people are bound in tradition. They focus on the past as his frame of reference. These are _________.

a) Laggard b) Late majority

c) Early majority d) None

91. The world is really shrinking day by day due to 3 t's they are ______.

a) Technology, Transport, Telecommunication

b) Transmitting, Transport, Telecommunication

c) Transport, Telecommunication, Techniques

d) Telecommunication, Technology, Transparency

92. Listening is separated into _____ levels.

a) 3 b) 5

c) 2 d) 4

93. N.A.L.P stands for ______.
    a) National Academy of Literate People
    b) National Academy of Literacy Programme
    c) National Adult Literacy Programme
    d) National Art Literate Programme
94. Socialization is possible only through ______.
    a) Communication
    b) Education
    c) Cultural promotion
    d) Maintaining relationship
95. Which method provides opportunities for face-to-face contact between the rural people & the extension workers?
    a) Group contact b) Individual contact
    c) Mass contact d) All
96. "The second tier of administration at the block level is ______.
    a) Panchayat Raj b) Panchayat samithi
    c) Zilla parishad d) Mahila mandal
97. ______ serves as a check on extension method.
    a) Evaluation b) Demonstration
    c) Co-operation d) Co-ordination
98. According to David barrio the purpose of communication is to ______.
    a) Influence b) Information
    c) Instruction d) Integration
99. The study of general principle of knowledge is ______.
    a) Physiological b) Sociology
    c) Philosophy d) Philanthropy
100. ______ is an important aspect of telecasting.
    a) Production b) Treatment
    c) Rehearsal d) Personal
101. Three types of credibility are ______.
    a) Present position, institute education, level education
    b) Interest, listening skill, cultural position
    c) Initial, derived, terminal
    d) None

102. ________ is not a visual aid.
a) Bulletin board b) Chalk board
c) Flannel graph d) Radio

103. Which is the moral fact of leadership?
a) Tact b) Initiative
c) Loyalty d) Integrity

104. Customs are socially prescribed form of behavior transmitted by
a) Tradition b) Belief
c) Culture d) None

105. Extension teaching should be based on the ______.
a) Needs of the people b) Needs of the extension workers
c) Needs of the teacher d) Needs of the doctors

106. Arya Samaj was founded by ________.
a) Raja Ram Mohan Roy b) Swami Dayanand Sarswati
c) Swami Satyanand d) Kabir

107. ________is essential for the efficient execution of entire programme.
a) Plan of work b) personality
c) demonstration d) all of these

108. In formal education the audience is _______.
a) Homogeneous b) Heterogeneous
c) Diversified d) All

109. ________ are useful for highlighting the main theme of a talk.
a) Posters b) Chart
c) Flip charts d) Flannel graph

110. The National literary Mission (NLM) launched in _______.
a) 1988 b) 1961
c) 1978 d) 1982

111. A new secretariat for agriculture was built in ______.
a) 1866 b) 1869
c) 1882 d) 1881

112. When the teaching is largely confined to the premises of the institution

a) Formal education b) Informal education

c) Extension education d) None

113. Interpersonal communication occurs only when ________.

a) An individual interacts with another person as a unique individual

b) Intimate conversion take place

c) Three or more people are communicating with each other at the same time

d) An individual converses with people these have no interest in knowing

114. Which of the following is advantage of campaign?

a) To build up community confidence

b) Relatively cheap

c) To reach people who are unable to attend extension meetings

d) All of these

115. The management of public affairs of a government is known as ________.

a) Evaluation b) Administration

c) Communication d) None

116. ________ is not an extension method.

a) Bulletin b) Individual contact

c) Group contact d) Mass contact

117. ________ is the chief characteristic of lecture method.

a) An organized presentation

b) Discussion

c) To adopt practically all lines of subject matter

d) None

118. In which type of education there is a fixed or predecided curriculum?

a) Extension education

b) Home Science extension education

c) Formal education

d) Informal education

119. Buzz sessions are also called as

a) Philips
b) Hubble system
c) Forum
d) Debate

120. Changes in the action of his hands must precedes ________.

a) Changes of attitudes
b) Change in mind
c) Changes of feeling
d) Changes of thinking

121. The active listening can ________.

a) Promotes poor listening
b) Enhances physical distraction
c) Facilitate problem solving
d) All

122. Representative members are chosen by ________.

a) Delegate groups
b) Locality groups
c) voluntary groups
d) involuntary groups

123. Learners are taught directly by the teachers then this education is known as _______.

a) Grow more food industries
b) Grow more food campaign
c) Growth of agricultural foods
d) None

124. The key person of the community development programme is _____.

a) Development officer
b) Manager
c) Gram sevak
d) All of these

125. ______________ demonstrated the transmission and reception of message.

a) G.Marconi
b) Hartoz
c) Maxwell
d) Watson

126. The extension approaches uses the extension teaching methods for _______.

a) Encourage the people
b) Support the people
c) Educating the people
d) Promote the people

127. What may be the result of the proper mixture of intelligence, emotional control and vision?

a) Good judgment
b) Good management
c) Good administration
d) Good skills

128. ________ can be used very effectively to build up a story or an explanation.

a) Flip chart b) Charts

c) Flannel graph d) Slides

129. The main function of extension education is to disseminate ________.

a) Information to people b) Money to people

c) Food to people d) None

130. A flannel graph of ______ size can be used to tell a story.

a) 10-20 inches b) 20-30 inches

c) 30-40 inches d) 40-50 inches

131. The most cheap and convenient material to use with flannel is ________

a) Bloating paper b) Carbon paper

c) A4 paper d) A3 paper

132. Local teachers are used for training and dissemination of knowledge in ________.

a) Formal education b) Extension education

c) Both a and b d) None

133. A leader who presides when the group is conducting business is ________.

a) Group executive b) Group planner

c) Group teacher d) Group educator

134. In which type of education there is no fixed curriculum?

a) Informal education b) Extension education

c) Both a and b d) Formal education

135. Formal education is ________.

a) Class-oriented b) Subject centered

c) Degree-oriented d) All

136. Those people who actually initiate action within the group, regardless of whether they hold an elected officer or not are ________.

a) Executive b) Top administrator

c) Subordinate staff d) Operation leader

137. In extension education the audience is ________.

a) Heterogeneous b) Homogeneous

c) Identical d) Both b and c

138. Which one of the following is the objective of office calls?

a) To build confidence

b) Select local leaders, demonstrators

c) To acquire new skill

d) To arrange timely supplies and services

139. Extension education helps in bringing about _______.

a) Friendliness b) Happiness

c) Interest d) Cultural development

140. Who is the intended receiver of message

a) Communication b) Audience

c) Decoder d) Encoder

141. Extension education is practical, field and ______.

a) Problem-oriented b) Teacher oriented

c) Theoretical d) Class-oriented

142. Harmonious adjustment is intended as ______

a) Planning b) Evaluation

c) Controlling d) Co-ordination

143. Number of flash cards used to educate the public is ______.

a) 10-11 b) 12-14

c) 10-12 d) 7-10

144. Feed back is the mirror of ______.

a) Channel b) Medium

c) Communication d) Stereotyping

145. The more informal and personal relationship in rural areas is ________.

a) Leadership pattern b) Social control

c) Social solidarity d) Social pattern

146. An example of communication channel is ______.

a) Noise b) Feed back

c) Face to face conversation d) Context

147. Extension is a two-way process where the extension agent transfers ________.

a) Money b) Rewards

c) Funds d) Knowledge and ideas

148. Practices and ceremonies are ____________

a) Rituals b) Mores

c) Taboo d) Folkways

149. ________ contains a series of pictures with or without words.

a) Black board b) Leaflets

c) Flannel graps d) Flip charts

150. When the teaching is largely outside the four walls of the institution then it is called _______.

a) Extension education b) Formal education

c) Both a and b d) None

151. In the communication process, to encode means to ______.

a) Interpret a code

b) Speak to large groups of people

c) Block a pathway between the sender and receiver of a message

d) Translate ideas into a code

152. _____ is the simplest functional unit of culture.

a) Cultural trait b) Ethos

c) Ethocentrism d) All of these

153. The point of origin of the message is

a) Source b) Message

c) Channels d) Receivers

154. Lay leaders are also called as ______.

a) Operational leaders b) Professional leaders

c) Administrative leaders d) Local leaders

155. Theory of human motivation was set forth by

a) Maslow b) Simon

c) Rogers d) Olmsted

156. The method extensively used to present authoritative information to integrates ideas is

a) Office call b) Lecture methods

c) Meeting d) Demonstration

157. Members of audience listen in terms of their

a) Interests b) Motivation

c) Memory d) Intelligence

158. Lecture method is generally called a

a) Debate b) Forum

c) Discussion d) Role play

159. One of the chief characteristics of the "lecture method" is

a) To adopt practically all lines of subject matter

b) Resource person are needed

c) An organized presentation

d) To provide for social and recreation; features

160. The group contact is also known as__________.

a) Method demonstration b) Home visit

c) Personal letter d) Observation plots

161. In group discussion, the size of the group should never exceed

a) 30 persons b) 40 persons

c) 25 persons d) 35 persons

162. The role of members in the group is to__________

a) Get balanced participation

b) Test all thinking by critical analysis

c) Give a final summary of discussions

d) All of these

163. Any timely information that interests a number of persons is

a) News articles b) Circular letters

c) Leaflets d) All of these

164. If people are against something, their negativeness can be transferred into being for something is known as

a) Channeling grips b) Trial

c) Exploiting crisis d) Past experiences

165. Micro teaching is based on

a) Theory b) Programmed learning

c) Computer assistance d) All

166. Participation of two teams, one representing the affirmative, the other the negative side of the question is

a) Debate b) Symposium

c) Panel d) Forum

167. If it is a decision debate, there is the temptation for the debate to become highly

a) Decorative b) Antagonistic

c) Temptative d) Controversial

168. A short series of lectures usually by 2 to 5 speakers is known as

a) Debate b) Symposium

c) Buzz sessions d) Panel

169. An informal conversation put on for the benefit of the audience, by a small group of speakers, usually from 2 to 8 in number is

a) Panel b) Forum

c) Symposium d) Debate

170. In which do the panel members hold a conversation among themselves on the topic, with questions and comments going from one member to another member?

a) Set-speech panel b) Conversation panel

c) Question-answer panel d) None of the above

171. In __________, each one makes a prepared speech.

a) Set-speech panel b) Question-answer panel

c) Teaching panel d) Conventional panel

172. The purposes of news articles are to

a) Adopt a new practice

b) Convey information to general public

c) Stimulate interest in a subject

d) All of these

173. A tool for giving information and entertainment is

a) Bulletin b) Circular letter

c) Radio d) News letter

174. An experimental programme called satellite television instructional experiment has been taken up in the year

a) 1970 b) 1990

c) 1975 d) 1985

175. Loosely organized and conjoined grouping of people with a common interest is ________.

a) Crowd b) Public

c) Mob d) None

176. An intensive teaching activity undertaken at an opportune time for brief period is

a) Radio b) Television

c) News article d) Campaign

177. One of the advantages of the campaign is

a) Relatively cheap

b) To build up community confidence

c) To reach people who are unable to attend extension meeting

d) Feasibility to do other things while listening

178. One of the strong points of individual contacts is

a) To increase confidence

b) To satisfy basic urge of people for social contacts

c) More effective in stimulating action than mass contacts

d) None of these

179. The factor influencing the choice of extension method is

a) Size of audience b) Age of the audience

c) Skills of the audience d) Attitude of audience

180. An "editing" of reality, differing from the original size in complexity is known as

a) Demonstration b) Contrived experience

c) Dramatized experiences d) None of these

181. ________ is often the most effective teaching aid.

a) Real object
b) Black board
c) Bulletins
d) Circular letters

182. A person in social interaction within a geographical area constitutes ________.

a) State
b) Region
c) Country
d) Community

183. Judging the values of something means

a) Co-ordination
b) Supervision
c) Planning
d) Evaluation

184. Co-ordinating is ________.

a) Harmonious adjustment
b) Co-operation
c) Friendliness
d) Evaluation

185. Agricultural universities were started on ________.

a) 1963
b) 1964
c) 1962
d) 1961

186. The Indian council of agricultural research was established in ______.

a) 1952
b) 1925
c) 1929
d) 1961

187. Sevagram attempt was started in ______.

a) 1921
b) 1920
c) 1980
d) 1981

188. Block development officer is a functionary created by the ______.

a) Private development programme
b) Community development programme
c) Government development programme
d) State development programme

189. Shriniketan project was established in the year of _____.

a) 1920
b) 1921
c) 1931
d) 1946

190. _________ allows colour photograph which will be very helpful in presentation.

a) Chart b) Black board

c) Leaflets d) Slides

191. Films used for educational purpose in motion-pictures is

a) 70mm b) 35mm

c) 16mm d) 8mm

192. Scales that show how people feel towards things

a) Attitude scales b) Knowledge tact

c) Interest checks d) Case history

193. The Etowah Pilot Project came into existence in _____.

a) 1961 b) 1958

c) 1940 d) 1948

194. Non-human resources include_____.

a) Money b) Skills

c) Knowledge d) Energy

195. Y.M.C.A was started in 1921 by_______.

a) Mahatma Gandhi b) Spencer Hatch

c) F.L.Brayne d) Albert Mayer

196. Sevagram attempt was started under the guidance of ______.

a) Rabindranath Tagore b) Elmhirst

c) Mahatma Gandhi d) None

197. The method which is concerned primarily with obtaining choice in interpersonal relation is _______.

a) Social relation b) Sociometry

c) Social work d) Social group

198. The three-tier system of the panchayat raj includes _____.

a) Village panchayat b) Zilla parishad

c) Panchayat samithi d) All of above

199. Who is the first deputy chairman of planning commission?

a) Sri V.T Krishnamachari b) Shree S.K. Dey

c) Albert Mayer d) Hatch

200. The Gurgaon attempt was organized by ______.
   a) Mahatma Gandhi b) Rabindranath Tagore
   c) F.L.Brayne d) Elmhirst
201. The objective of the rural development programme is to develop
   a) People's participation b) People's organization
   c) People's administration d) People's leadership
202. The method used with every other material on the "cone of experience" is
   a) Recording b) Still pictures
   c) Visual d) Verbal
203. An essentially recognizable imitation of the original work is known as ________.
   a) Model b) Specimen
   c) Mock-up d) Object
204. Real objects taken out of their natural settings are ____________.
   a) Mock-ups b) Specimens
   c) Objects d) Models
205. Non photographic reconstructions of reality are
   a) Illustrations b) Specimens
   c) Models d) All of the above
206. Roll up chalk boards are usually made of
   a) Heavy cloth b) Leather board
   c) Fibre board d) Heavy card boards
207. A simple inexpensive device that can be placed either outdoor or indoor is
   a) Chalk board b) Flannel graph
   c) Bulletin board d) Radio
208. Rigid chalk boards can be made of
   a) Oil cloth b) Heavy cloth
   c) Plywood d) Canvas
209. Written messages which are hidden by strips of thick cardboard form is known as
   a) Time charts b) Job charts
   c) Stream charts d) Pull charts

210. Charts used to show organizational or administrative relationships are
   a) Pull charts b) Bar charts
   c) Flow charts d) Table charts
211. Charts used to compare quantities at different circumstances are
   a) Bar charts b) Pictorial charts
   c) Line charts d) Pie charts
212. Charts consisting of a series of individual charts which are tacked together and hung on a supporting stand are
   a) Table chart b) Flip chart
   c) Tree chart d) Over-lay chart
213. Charts consisting of a number of illustrated sheets which can be placed one over the other conveniently
   a) Over-lay charts b) Pull charts
   c) Strip tease charts d) Flow charts
214. Which of the following is in the shape of circle?
   a) Time chart b) Pie chart
   c) Organization chart d) Job chart
215. Charts that are particularly useful in showing trends and relationships are
   a) Line charts b) Stream charts
   c) Time charts d) Pictorial charts
216. It is a visual symbol made with the help of lines and geometrical forms without pictorial elements to explain mostly a process or parts of something
   a) Graph b) Diagram
   c) Photograph d) Pictures
217. A statement of situation, objectives, problems and solutions is
   a) Extension methods b) Extension programme
   c) Extension education d) Extension projection
218. To solve a problem _________ is required
   a) Change agent b) Client systems
   c) Both a and b d) None of the above
219. Which of the following does not constitute understanding?
   a) Attitude b) Skills
   c) Knowledge of facts d) Personality

220. Changes in the action of his hands must precede
  a) Changes in thinking b) Changes of feelings
  c) Changes of mid d) Changes of attitudes

221. The non-formal system of education is referred as _______.
  a) Adult education b) Extension education
  c) Both a and b d) Distance education

222. Authority is the power to make _______.
  a) Strong b) Decision
  c) Ability d) None

223. I.A.D.P is commonly called as _______.
  a) Community programme b) Package programme
  c) Cropping programme d) Area programme

224. The theory assumes that certain person is born to be leader is_______.
  a) Social theory b) Physiological theory
  c) Psychological theory d) Biological theory

225. Secondary social groups has ______.
  a) Little intimacy and limited involvement
  b) Little intimacy and limited group
  c) More intimacy and limited involvement
  d) More intimacy and more group

226. The extension officers are also called as _______.
  a) Development officers b) Block officers
  c) Extension staff specialist d) Subject matter specialists

227. The National Adult Education programme was launched on 2nd October _______.
  a) 1957 b) 1964
  c) 1978 d) 1975

228. For bringing attitudinal changes in adults, the most suitable method is _______.
  a) Home visit b) Group meeting
  c) Method demonstrations d) Role play

229. Inclusive education means _______.

a) Following same schedule for all children

b) Educating disabled and normal children in the same school

c) Educating children in their neighbourhood school

d) All

230. The principle of learning includes _______.

a) Desire
b) Conviction
c) Learning should be meaningful
d) Action

231. Who is the chairman of the development committee?

a) Planning officer
b) Collector
c) Development officer
d) Administrative officer

232. The leader of Bhoodan movement was _________.

a) Mahatma Gandhi
b) Acharya Vinoba Bhave
c) Rabindranath Tagore
d) Elimhirst

233. Shriniketan attempt was started by Rabindranath Tagore in ________.

a) Haryana
b) Karnataka
c) Bengal
d) Kerala

234. BMN strands for _______.

a) Basic Minimum Need
b) Basic Maximum Need
c) Ban Minimum Need
d) Basic Minor Need

235. The first organized effort through community development programme was taken in ________.

a) 1952
b) 1953
c) 1954
d) 1955

236. The first person who adopts a new idea____________

a) Receiver
b) Learners
c) Early adopters
d) Innovators

237. Which is a non-projected aid?

a) Overhead projector
b) Bulletin board
c) Opaque projector
d) Slide projector

238. Chairman of Zilla Parishad is elected by ______.

a) Sarpanchas
b) Extensive officer
c) Extension workers
d) Development officer

239. LCD strands for _______.

a) Local Compact Disc b) Liquid Crystal Display

c) Long Compact Display d) Liquid Compact Disc

240. The opinion that "our aim should be to produce men who possess both culture and expect knowledge" given by _______.

a) Prof. A.H. Whitehead b) Montessori

c) Froebel d) Marx

241. How do we get knowledge and how can we be sure it is true and not error? This area of philosophy is called ________.

a) Neurology b) Epistemology

c) Beyond Philosophy d) None of the above

242. All levels of education are provided from the nursery to the University stage in ______.

a) Ashram at Pondicherry b) Brahmo Samaj

c) Shantiniketan d) Arya Samaj

243. In today's society school should give ______.

a) Ornamental base b) Vocational base

c) Both a & b d) None of the above

244. Who formed Brahmo Samaj?

a) Guru Nanak b) Kabir

c) Ramanand d) Raja Ram Mohan Roy

245. A method to identify community leader is _______.

a) Group discussion b) Interview

c) Lottery method d) Written test

246. Annie Besant inspired the opening of schools in many cities in ________.

a) End of nineteenth century b) Early nineteenth century

c) Early twentieth century d) End of twentieth century

247. Democratic decentralization is known as _______.

a) Panchayat Samithi b) Panchayat Raj

c) Zilla Parishad d) Mahila Mandal

248. Ahimsa & Truth in Gandhiji's opinion is ________.

a) Two side of a coin

b) Have no relation between the two

c) Can't translate

d) Can't inter-wined

249. The 1968 national policy adopted by the Indian Government laid stress on which of the following aspect of teacher's education?

a) Adequate emoluments and academic freedom for teachers

b) Travel allowance and family pensions for teachers

c) In-service training and correspondence education for teachers.

d) Promotion and retirement facilities for teachers

250. The objective of the Etawah Pilot Project is ________.

a) To awaken the desire of rural people and to make them laborious.

b) To develop the feeling of self-confidence, co-operation and mass participation

c) To develop the agriculture and animal husbandry

d) All of the above

Answers

1. a	2. c	3. a	4. a	5. c	6. a	7. d	8. c	9. b	10. b
11. a	12. a	13. b	14. c	15. d	16. a	17. a	18. c	19. b	20. d
21. d	22. c	23. a	24. d	25. d	26. c	27. b	28. b	29. a	30. c
31. d	32. b	33. a	34. a	35. b	36. c	37. d	38. b	39. d	40. a
41. d	42. b	43. b	44. d	45. a	46. b	47. d	48. a	49. c	50. d
51. d	52. a	53. d	54. d	55. d	56. b	57. b	58. c	59. c	60. a
61. b	62. b	63. b	64. c	65. b	66. a	67. c	68. d	69. c	70. d
71. a	72. b	73. d	74. d	75. b	76. d	77. a	78. a	79. c	80. c
81. d	82. c	83. b	84. a	85. d	86. d	87. d	88. d	89. c	90. a
91. a	92. a	93. c	94. a	95. b	96. b	97. a	98. a	99. c	100. c
101. c	102. d	103. d	104. a	105. a	106. b	107. a	108. a	109. a	110. a
111. d	112. a	113. a	114. a	115. b	116. d	117. a	118. c	119. b	120. b
121. c	122. b	123. b	124. c	125. a	126. c	127. a	128. c	129. a	130. c

131. a	132. b	133. a	134. c	135. d	136. d	137. a	138. d	139. d	140. b
141. a	142. d	143. c	144. c	145. b	146. c	147. d	148. a	149. d	150. a
151. d	152. a	153. a	154. d	155. a	156. b	157. a	158. b	159. c	160. a
161. a	162. d	163. d	164. a	165. a	166. a	167. b	168. b	169. a	170. b
171. a	172. d	173. c	174. c	175. b	176. d	177. b	178. a	179. a	180. b
181. a	182. d	183. d	184. a	185. d	186. c	187. b	188. b	189. b	190. d
191. c	192. a	193. d	194. a	195. b	196. c	197. b	198. d	199. a	200. c
201. a	202. d	203. a	204. b	205. d	206. a	207. c	208. c	209. d	210. c
211. a	212. b	213. a	214. b	215. a	216. c	217. b	218. c	219. c	220. c
221. c	222. b	223. b	224. d	225. a	226. d	227. c	228. d	229. b	230. c
231. b	232. b	233. c	234. a	235. a	236. d	237. b	238. a	239. b	240. a
241. b	242. a	243. b	244. d	245. a	246. a	247. b	248. a	249. a	250. d

8

Research Methodology

1. Cronbach's alpha reliability is:

   a) The correlation of half of the items with the total participants

   b) The correlation of each item with the sum of the items

   c) An average of all possible split-half reliabilities

   d) None of these

2. Internal reliability is:

   a) About how consistently all of the items in a scale measure the concept in question.

   b) About the consistently of a measure taken at two different points in time.

   c) About how a single individual's scores remain identical.

   d) About the increase or decrease in scores over time.

3. The research can be_______________

   a) Field setting research b) Laboratory research

   c) Simulation research d) Depends upon the environment

4. Which one of these characteristics would you expect not to give high test-retest reliability?

   a) Attention b) Dyslexia

   c) Intelligence d) Religious belief

5. Primary data can be collected through_______________

   a) Experimental b) Survey

   c) Both a and b d) None of these

6. Primary data are ____________

   a) Less reliable compared to secondary data

   b) Always more reliable compared to secondary data

   c) Depends on the care with which data have been collected

   d) None of these

7. Which of the following is a secondary data?

   a) Ordinary data b) Existing data

   c) Unimportant data d) Ordinal data

8. Secondary data are LEAST helpful to:

   a) Interpret tables b) Formulate hypotheses

   c) Develop questionnaires d) Evaluate new products

9. ____________ study determines frequency with which something occurs with something else.

   a) Diagnostic b) Experimental

   c) Descriptive d) None of these

10. The comparison with controlled group shows____________

    a) Occurrence of effect frequency

    b) Cause occurred before an effect or not

    c) Other factors determining conditions

    d) All of these

11. ____________ is known as purposive non-probability sampling.

    a) Subjective sampling b) Simple random sampling

    c) Stratified sampling d) All of these

12. Who stated, "Experimental design is simply observation under controlled conditions"?

    a) F. S. Chapin b) Vimal shah

    c) R.L Ackoff d) None of these

13. The interview method depends on individual researchers____________

    a) Ability b) Capability

    c) Communication d) Sensitivity to situation

14. Units of analysis and interpretation includes________

a) Co efficient b) Rates

c) Ratio and percentage d) None of these

15. Secondary data______________.

a) Should never be used

b) Should be used after careful scrutiny

c) No scrutiny is required while using it

d) None of these

16. Correlating between different versions of a test is known as________

a) Objectivity b) Alternate forms reliability

c) Test-retest reliability d) Split-half reliability

17. The number of questions in questionnaires should be__________

a) 15

b) 20

c) 50

d) As small as possible keeping in view the purpose of survey

18. "Research is a careful and critical query or examination in seeking facts or principles diligent investigation in order to ascertain something" was said by____________.

a) Webs tens international dictionary

b) Prot Clifford moody

c) Stephenson

d) F. Wittis

19. Specific qualities that should be present in research worker________

a) Knowledge of the subject, techniques of research

b) Personal taste in the study

c) Familiarity about the informants

d) All of these

20. Most governments in the world have statistical departments but they are unlikely to provide:
    a) Television programme viewing figures.
    b) General population census records
    c) Agricultural census results
    d) Housing statistics.
21. A predictive statement that relates an independent variable to a dependent variable ____.
    a) Objective b) Psychological variable
    c) Hypothesis d) Extraneous variable
22. While forming grouped frequency distribution, the number of classes should be________________
    a) Less than 5 b) More than 20
    c) Between 4 and 10 d) Between 5 and 15
23. Diagram and graphs are tools of______________
    a) Analysis b) Collection of data
    c) Presentation d) None of these
24. Which of the following are problem in way of research____________
    a) Existence of good investigator
    b) Collections of information is depends on others
    c) Analysis of data
    d) All of these
25. In a two dimensional diagram ____________ is considered
    a) Only height b) Only width
    c) Both height and width d) Height, width and thickness
26. Which of the following is the most unstable average______________
    a) Mode b) Median
    c) Arithmetic mean d) Geometric mean
27. The positional measure of central tendency is________________
    a) Median b) Arithmetic mean
    c) Geometric mean d) None of these

28. The Coefficient of correlation is_______________

a) Can be less than 1 b) Can be more than 1

c) Varies between± 1 d) Has no limits

29. The measure of variation that is least affected by extreme observation is _______________

a) Mean deviation b) Standard deviation

c) Quartile deviation d) All of these

30. Researcher should find the answer to research questions___________-

a) Validity b) Objectively

c) Accurately d) All of the above

31. For dealing with qualitative data the best average is___________-

a) Arithmetic mean b) Median

c) Mode d) Geometric mean

32. When one regression coefficient is negative, the other would be______

a) Bivariate b) Positive

c) Zero d) None of thee

33. There will be only one regression line in case of two variable, if______

a) R=0 b) R=+1

c) R= - 1 d) R is either +1 or -1

34. While drawing a scatter diagram if all points appear to form a straight line going down ward from left to right, then it is inferred that there is_______________.

a) Simple positive correlation b) Perfect positive correlation

c) Perfect negative correlation d) No correlation

35. Large sample theory is applicable when___________

a) N=30 b) N> 30

c) N< 30 d) All of these

36. The x^2 test was devised by _______________

a) Gauss b) Laplace

c) Karl Pearson d) None of these

37. Analysis of variance techniques originated in________

a) Industrial research b) Biological research

c) Agrarian research d) None of these

38. Latin square are most widely used in the field of______

a) Industry b) Medicine

c) Astronomy d) Agriculture

39. The process of sampling involves________ elements

a) Selecting the sample

b) Collecting the information

c) Making an inference about the population

d) All of these

40. The probability sampling is also known as__________

a) Random sampling b) Non-random sampling

c) Judgment sampling d) Quota sampling

41. The design tell us about the universe of the study it means__________

a) How many cases will be covered

b) What manner will these cases be picked

c) How will cases be identified

d) All of these

42. Karl Pearson's coefficient of skewness

a) Is always positive

b) Is always negative

c) Can be both positive and negative

d) Cannot be zero

43. Who stated, "The research design is the plan structure and strategy of investigation conceived so as to obtain answer to research question and control variance"?

a) Fred. N Kerlinger b) R.L Achoff

c) E.A. Suchaman d) Karl Pearson

44. Study which accurately portray the characteristics of a particular situation or groups or individual is ____________

a) Exploratory b) Descriptive

c) Experimental d) None of these

45. The comparison with control groups show ____________

a) Occurrence of effect frequency

b) Cause an occurred before an effect or not

c) Other factors determining conditions

d) All of these

46. Which one of the following is non probability sampling method?

a) Judgment sampling b) Convenience sampling

c) Quota sampling d) All of these

47. Bias is caused due to ____________

a) Faulty process of selection b) Faulty work during the collection

c) Faulty methods of analysis d) All of these

48. If A is necessary condition for B but B never occurs unless A occurred. Such a relationship is also known as____________.

a) Alternative condition b) Producer – product relationship

c) A cause d) None of these

49. Which of following comes under restricted random sampling method____________

a) Cluster sampling b) Convenience sampling

c) Both a and b d) None of the above

50. Much of the development in the theory of probability is associated with the name of ____________

a) Karl Pearson b) Fisher

c) Bayes d) Gosset

51. ________ classification are usually listed in alphabetical order for easy reference

a) Chronological b) Geographical

c) Qualitative d) Quantitative

52. __________ study aim at gaining familiarity with a phenomena or which aim at achieving insight into the phenomena or study which deals with formulation of more precise a research problem or developing hypotheses.

a) Experimental b) Descriptive
c) Exploratory d) All of these

53. In chronological classification data are classified on the basis of ______

a) Time b) Attributes
c) Religion d) None of these

54. The individual items in a population are called ________

a) Sample b) Elementary units
c) Frame d) Cluster

55. Which of the following is used to obtain the desired data __________.

a) Survey b) Sample
c) Secondary data d) None of these

56. When population under investigation is infinite, we should use the __________ method

a) Census b) Sample
c) Either census or sample d) None of these

57. Who said regarding statistical methods, "nothing else was more important but mathematics applied to human facts".

a) Bogardus b) Galton
c) Gidding d) None of these

58. Sampling errors are present only in ______________

a) Sample survey
b) Complete enumeration survey
c) Both census and sample surveys
d) Neither sample nor census survey

59. __________ is most widely used for graphical presentation of frequency distribution.

a) Frequency polygon b) Histogram
c) Smoothed frequency curve d) Ogives

60. The term of errors in statistics refers to ________
  a) Mistakes
  b) Bias
  c) Difference between the value of a statistic and the corresponding parameter
  d) All of these

61. ________ errors are likely to be more in case of complete enumeration survey
  a) Non-sampling b) Sampling
  c) Both a and b d) Bias

62. Bar diagrams are ________ dimensional diagram
  a) One b) Two
  c) Three d) None of these

63. ________ are used to give quantitative information on a geographical basis
  a) Bar diagrams b) Simple bar diagram
  c) Cartogram d) Volume diagram

64. Volume diagrams are otherwise known as ________
  a) One dimensional diagram b) Two dimensional diagram
  c) There dimensional diagrams d) Pictographs

65. The variables we are trying to predict is called ________
  a) Dependent variables b) Independent variables
  c) Both a and b d) None of these

66. Yule's coefficient of association can be ________
  a) Greater than 1 b) Less than 1
  c) Cannot be zero d) Take any value between ± 1

67. Statistics is today needed for ________
  a) Data collection b) Tabulation of data
  c) Both a and b d) None of these

68. State which is / are true________________

a) The problem which are primarily of qualitative nature cannot be studied by quantitative method

b) Statistical method deals with number not with cause

c) Very few investigator and researcher are prepared to go to the field

d) All of these

69. The dependent variables is always denoted by____________-

a) X_1 b) X_2

c) X_3 d) Both b and c

70. Data are classified into ________________

a) Column and rows b) Column

c) Rows d) None of these

71. In a symmetrical distribution, mean is equal to ____________

a) Median b) Mode

c) Standard deviation d) None of these

72. The standard error provides an idea about the ____________ of sample

a) Unreliability b) Reliability

c) Both a and b d) None of these

73. Classification is the ________________ steps in tabulation

a) First b) Second

c) Third d) None of these

74. The heading of rows in a statistical table is known as____________

a) Title b) Stub

c) Caption d) All of these

75. ________________ is a computed measure of central tendency

a) Mean b) Median

c) Mode d) All of these

76. The value of ______________ can be determined graphically

a) Arithmetic mean b) Mode

c) Both a and b d) None of these

77. The graphical method can be used to solve ______

a) A linear programming problem with two decision variables

b) A linear programming problem with all integer data base

c) Any linear programming problem

d) A transportation problem with two origins and two destinations

78. ________ is the reciprocal of the arithmetic mean of the values

a) Geometric mean b) Harmonic mean

c) Both a and b d) None of these

79. An average alone is sufficient to understand the basic characteristic of ________

a) Symmetrical distribution b) Mean

c) Central tendency d) Frequency distribution

80. The term regression was first used by Karl Pearson in the year ______

a) 1980 b) 1972

c) 1990 d) None of these

81. The probability ranges from______________

a) 0-1 b) 0-2

c) 1 d) 0

82. To determine the frequency with which something occurs or is associated with something else is known as __________

a) Formulative research b) Descriptive research

c) Diagnostic research d) Exploratory research

83. To test a hypothesis of a casual relationship between variable is known as ____________ research

a) Hypothesis testing b) Exploratory

c) Formulative d) Descriptive

84. Combination of cluster and stratified random sampling are termed as ____________

a) Purposive sampling b) Stage sampling

c) Quota sampling d) None of these

85. Which of the following is considered as motivating factor in research?
    a) Desire to understand cause and effect of widespread social problems
    b) Existence of sequence or low in activities
    c) Possibility of detached study
    d) Possibility of representative data
86. Research is ________________
    a) Searching again and again
    b) Finding solution to any problem
    c) Working in a scientific way to search for truth of any problem
    d) None of the above
87. The most appropriate statistical test for analyzing qualitative data is ____________
    a) Pearson's b) Sign test
    c) T-test d) F-test
88. The most appropriate statistical test for analyzing quantitative data is ____________
    a) Chi square test b) T-test
    c) Sign test d) All of these
89. An example of cross sectional study is____________
    a) Comparing individuals of various ages at the same time
    b) Careful description by the researcher
    c) On that requires no manipulation
    d) Continued observation of the same individual
90. A common test in research demands much priority on ____________-
    a) Reliability b) Unreliability
    c) Objectivity d) All of the above
91. The reasoning where we start with certain particular statements and conclude with a universal statement is called____________.
    a) Deductive reasoning b) Inductive reasoning
    c) Abnormal reasoning d) Transcendental reasoning

92. Which of the following is incorrect statement?

a) Hypothesis is a proposed explanation for phenomenon

b) A hypothesis is made on the basis of limited evidence as a starting point for further investigations

c) A hypothesis is a basis for reasoning without any assumption of its truth

d) Scientific hypothesis is a scientific theory

93. According to John Dewey scientific attitude is linked with________

a) Curiosity b) Fertile imagination

c) Love of experimental enquiry d) All of these

94. Sir Francis Galton states this "an inherent stimulus to climb the path that leads to knowledge with strength to reach the summit" about________

a) Imagination b) Scientific attitude

c) Perseverance d) Grasping power

95. State which is /are true __________

a) A research design will always help us in knowing successive stages

b) Research design will help identifying the importance of each step in the whole scheme of things, Design will also help in finding out what total time the study is likely to take and what time each step in the study is likely to consume

c) The design helps in making the research know as to why is he studying the issue and what type of data will be needed , how data will be found

d) All of these

96. The drawbacks of qualitative methods is / are

a) Subjectivity b) Individual oriented

c) Data not reliable and precise d) All of these

97. The difficulties of field work could be __________

a) Unhygienic conditions

b) Heavy rainfalls

c) Jungles and people will not cooperate

d) All of these

98. "Interviewing has become of greater importance in contemporary research because of reassessment of qualitative research" was said by

a) Goode and Hatt b) Bogardiss

c) Galton d) Gibbons

99. Who stated "The Interviewer is perhaps the most ubiquitous method of obtaining information from the people" __________.

a) Goode and Hatt b) Fred N. Kerlinger

c) Gibbons d) Bogardiss

100. What could be kept in mind regarding a questionnaire __________?

a) Size b) Appearance

c) Clarity and catching d) All of these

101. The advantage of questionnaire method could be__________

a) Low cost and large coverage b) Repetitive information

c) Rapidly d) All of these

102. Non structured questionnaire often known as interview guide is used for __________ interviews

a) Focused b) Depth

c) Non–directive d) All of these

103. The interview method depends on individual researcher's__________

a) Ability b) Capability

c) Communication d) Sensitivity to situation

104. The defects of questionnaire method could possibly be__________

a) Ambiguous format b) Half hearted information

c) Biased interpretation d) All of these

105. Questionnaire could pose a limitations because of__________

a) Unavailability, incomplete entries

b) Manipulated entries, lack of personal care

c) Impossibility of in-depth response

d) All of these

106. Techniques of interview involves a steps of ____________

a) Establishing contact, starting an interview

b) Securing rapport, recall

c) Probe question, encouragement

d) All of these

107. Structured questionnaire contains ____________ questions

a) Definite
b) Concrete
c) Pre-ordinate
d) All of these

108. The sources of case data is/are ____________

a) Diaries
b) Letters
c) Life history
d) All of these

109. In a descriptive or diagnostic study bias plays an important role , it can be checked by:

a) One answer structured question

b) No leading question asked

c) A sampling of group studied and data collection instruments pre-tested

d) All of these

110. Using different methods of collecting data, different sources of evidence, different tests and in some cases different interviewers, is known as what?

a) Triangulation
b) Transferability
c) Convergent validity
d) Reliability

111. The difference between descriptive and diagnostic design lies in ____________

a) Difference in field
b) Difference in hypothesis
c) Difference in objectives
d) All of these

112. The basic assumption in case study is /are ____________

a) Totally of the being
b) Underlying unity
c) Influence of time
d) All of these

113. Public opinion poll method sought replies like__________

a) Yes /no
b) I do not know
c) Possibility
d) All of these

114. The basis of sampling is on the assumption__________

a) Underlying homogeneity amidst complexity
b) Possibility of representative selection
c) Absolute accuracy not essential
d) All of these

115. An example of cross-sectional study is__________.

a) Comparing individuals of various ages at the same time
b) Careful description by the researcher
c) On that requires no manipulation
d) Continued observation of the same individuals

116. A predictive statement that relates an independent variable to a dependent variable__________

a) Hypothesis
b) Objective
c) Extraneous variable
d) Psychological variable

117. Which of the following are associated with behavioral observation?

a) Non verbal analysis
b) Linguistic analysis
c) Spatial analysis
d) All of these

118. Which of the following is the first step in starting the research process?

a) Searching sources of information to locate problem
b) Searching for solution to the problem
c) Identification of problem
d) Searching for solution to the problem

119. Which of the following variables cannot be expressed in quantitative terms?

a) Socio economic status
b) Marital status
c) Numerical aptitude
d) Professional attitude

120. In the process of conducting research, formulation of hypothesis is followed by_________.

a) Statement of objectives b) Analysis of data

c) Selection of research tools d) Collection of data

121. Action research means __________

a) A longitudinal research

b) An applied research

c) A research initiated to solve an immediate problem

d) A research with socio economic objectives

122. The essential qualities of a researcher are __________

a) Spirit of free enquiry

b) Reliance on observation and evidence

c) Systematization or theorizing of knowledge

d) All of the above

123. A research paper is brief report of research work based on________

a) Primary data only b) Secondary data only

c) Both a and b d) None of the above

124. Which of the statements are true __________

a) There are no limits to the value of r

b) If r is negative, both the variables are decreasing

c) Correlation always signifies a cause and effect relationship between the variables

d) Spurious correlation implies real relationship the variables

125. In t-test when separate samples are selected in two groups in one population or in two populations, the test used is

a) One-tailed test b) Two-tailed test

c) Analysis of variance d) All of these

126. The method of Randomization is

a) Lottery or coin method

b) Blind folded or dice method

c) Tippet s table of irregular members

d) All the above

127. Which is the basic assumption in research?
   a) Add new knowledge to the existing, store and remove inapplicable theory
   b) Study inter-disciplinary problems in right perceptions
   c) Curiosity about unknown
   d) Existence of cause and effect relationship
128. Which of the following states the qualities of a good research?
   a) Systematic b) Logical
   c) Empirical d) All of these
129. The researcher must arrange his idea in order and write them in the form of an experimental plan is called as_______.
   a) Research design b) Research plan
   c) Both a & b d) None of these
130. Which of the following sampling methods is based on probability?
   a) Convenience sampling b) Stratified random sampling
   c) Purposive sampling d) Quota sampling
131. ________ sample is known as chance sampling.
   a) Systematic sampling b) Simple random sampling
   c) Deliberate sampling d) None of these
132. The limitation of the two-group randomized design is usually eliminated within the _____ design.
   a) Randomized block design
   b) Random replication design
   c) Two-group simple randomized design
   d) None of these
133. Which of the following is basic assumption in research?
   a) Existence of cause and effect relationship
   b) Existence of sequence or law in activities
   c) Possibility of detached study
   d) All of these

134. The number of families and members of each family male/female ratio in village is an example of

a) Definite universe b) Real universe

c) Hypothetical universe d) None

135. The characteristics of source list includes

1. Exhaustive 2. Valid

3. No repetition 4. Full information

a) 1,2,3,4 b) 1,2,3

c) 1,2 d) 1,4

136. Which is the specific quality of a good research worker?

a) Imagination

b) Knowledge of the subject, technique of research

c) Grasping power

d) Unbiased attitude

137. ______ research aims at finding a solution for an immediate problem facing a society or an industrial or business organization.

a) Fundamental b) Applied research

c) Descriptive d) Analytic

138. The number of families residing in a particular village or the number of students studying in a college or number of females and males serving in an office is an example of

1. Indefinite universe 2. Definite universe

a) Only 1 b) Only 2

c) Both 1 and 2 d) None

139. Disadvantages of stratified sampling are

a) Bias in sample

b) Proportion difficult in equal strata

c) Undue weight make the sample unrepresentative

d) All

140. The entire group from which sample is chosen is known as
   a) The population b) Universe
   c) Supply d) All
141. Who stated "A statistical sample is miniature picture or cross section of the entire group or aggregate from which the sample is taken."
   a) Goode and Hatt b) P.V. Young
   c) Gibbon d) Gosset .W.S
142. Dividing the field into several homogenous part is known as________.
   a) Blocking b) Variability
   c) Deliberating d) None of these
143. Probability samples are based on______.
   a) Simple random sampling b) Systematic sampling
   c) Stratified sampling d) All of these
144. _______ deals with the method of selecting the subjects.
   a) Statistical design b) Sampling design
   c) Both a & b d) None
145. In laboratory experiment the effect of manipulation of an independent variables upon the dependent variables is observed under ______.
   a) Controlled condition b) Uncontrolled condition
   c) Indirect condition d) None
146. Experiments with more than two factors at a time involve in ______.
   a) Simple factorial design b) Complex factorial design
   c) Varied sample design d) All of these
147. A variable that can be manipulated is ______.
   a) Dependent variable b) Independent variable
   c) Continuous variable d) Discrete variable
148. Arrange the following steps of research in correct sequence:
   1. Identification of research problem
   2. Listing of research objectives
   3. Collection of data
   4. Methodology

5. Data analysis
6. Results and Discussion

a) 1-2-3-4-5-6 b) 1-3-4-2-5-6
c) 2-1-3-4-5-6 d) 2-1-4-3-5-6

149. Who stated "The systematic method of discovering new facts or verifying old facts than sequences interrelationship casual explanations and the natural laws which govern them"?

a) F.A. Ogs b) Rodman And Morey
c) Stephenson d) P.V Young

150. The analysis of the Latin square design is very similar to the ______ techniques.

a) One way ANOVA b) Two-way ANOVA
c) Both a &b d) None

151. Who states "the design in the plan of study and as such it is planned in every study uncontrolled as well as controlled and subjective as well as objective"?

a) Stephenson b) Prof Clifford Moody
c) Rodman And Mordy d) Vimal Status

152. Mail questionnaire is less expensive than ______ method.

a) Panel technique b) Interview
c) Telephone survey d) Evolutionary method

153. Exploratory research studies are also termed as ____ research

a) Descriptive b) Formulative
c) Diagnostic d) All of these

154. If the items selected from each stratus is based on simple random sampling then it is known as______________.

a) Quota sampling b) Stratified random sampling
c) Multi stage sampling d) Sequential

155. "Law of comparative judgment" is developed by_____.

a) L.L Turnstone b) Morg
c) Redmen d) RothanSted

156. Which of the following is principle of experimental design?

a) Principle of replications b) Principle of randomization

c) Principle of local control d) All of these

157. Guttmann's coefficient of reproducibility is _______.

a) 1-e/n (N) b) 1-n/e (N)

c) 1-e/N (n) d) e/n (N)-1

158. Data obtained by basis of certain attributes are known as _____.

a) Statistics of variables b) Statistics of attributes

c) Class magnitude d) Class intervals

159. Defining the research problem is the preparation of the design of the research project is properly known as _______.

a) Research problem b) Research design

c) Research hypothesis d) None

160. A field experiment is very similar to a ______ experiment.

a) Laboratory b) Ex post facto studies

c) Formulative studies d) Exploratory

161. A complete enumeration of all the items in the population is known as_________.

a) Universe inquiry b) Population inquiry

c) Census inquiry d) All of these

162. Which of the following is formal experimental design?

a) Completely randomized design

b) Randomized block design

c) Latin square design

d) All of these

163. Survey research may be defined as a technique whereby the research studies the whole population with respect to certain _______ variables.

a) Sociological b) Psychological

c) Both a & b d) None

164. Which of the following statement is wrong?

a) Good research is systematic b) Good research is logical

c) Good research is empirical d) Good research is replicable

165. Which of the following is classification of measurement scale?

a) Nominal scale b) Ordinal scale

c) Interval scale d) All of these

166. Scalogram analysis can be used for ______.

a) Telephone b) Personal

c) Mail survey d) All of these

167. The experimental study is ______.

a) Antagonistic b) Ex-post facto

c) Antagonistic to ex-post facto d) None

168. Which one of the following is the stable measure of dispersion?

a) Standard deviation b) Range

c) Quartile deviation d) Average deviation

169. Standard deviation is worked out as ______.

a) $(\sigma) = (x_{i-} x)^{-2}/n$ b) $(\sigma) = \sqrt{}(x_{i-} x)^{2}/n$

c) $(\sigma) =$ "$(x_{i-} x)^{-2}$"$/n$ d) $(\sigma) = \sqrt{}(x_{i-} x)^{-2}$

170. Independent variable not manipulated is called as ______.

a) Non experimental design

b) Experimental testing research

c) Non experimental hypothesis testing research

d) Experimental hypothesis

171. Independent variable for an experimental research is also termed as__________.

a) Manipulated variables b) Experimental variables

c) Treatment variables d) All of these

172. ______ is the lowest inference descriptor of all because it uses the participant's own words

a) Participant feedback b) Data triangulation

c) A verbatim d) Investigator triangulation

173. Who defined "research as a systematical effort to gain new knowledge?

a) Redman and Mory b) Stephenson

c) Slesinger d) Clifford woody

174. Correlation can be studied through ______.

a) Cross tabulation

b) Charles Spearman's coefficient of correlation

c) Karl Pearson's coefficient of correlation

d) All of these

175. Researcher in ______ science has the advantages to describe variables in ratio scale.

a) Physical science b) Behavioral science

c) Both a & b d) None

176. A good design is characterized by ______.

a) Flexible b) Appropriate

c) Efficient d) All of these

177. ______ is based on the normal probability distribution and is used for judging the significance of several statically measure particularly the mean.

a) χ^2 test b) Z-test

c) t-test d) F-test

178. In survey method of research the mail questionnaire is used in ______ research.

a) Education b) Sociological

c) Both a &b d) None

179. Whose name is associated with experimental design?

a) Rotham Sted b) Redman

c) Mory d) R.A Fishers

180. ______ is concerned with broad underlying feeling or motivations or with the course of individual life experience.

a) Focused interview b) Clinical interview

c) Non directive interview d) Unstructured interview

181. ______ design relates to the condition under the observation.

a) Statistical
b) Observational
c) Operational
d) All of these

182. Research design refers to the procedures for____.

a) Collection of data
b) Analysis
c) Both a & b
d) None

183. Theoretical framework already available, which can be either be accepted or refused, is called _____ method.

a) Library method
b) Experimental method
c) Field study method
d) Both a & b

184. The members are compared as multiples of one another in________

a) Ratio data
b) Nominal data
c) Ordinal data
d) Interval data

185. Scalogram analysis refer to the procedure for determining whether a set of items form a _______.

a) One-dimensional scale
b) Undimensional scale
c) Dimensional scale
d) None

186. Probability sampling under restricted sampling techniques may result in complex random sampling design called as____

a) Systematic sampling
b) Stratified sampling
c) Mixed sampling design
d) Random sampling

187. Every practical design consist of______

a) Sample design
b) Observation design
c) Statistical design
d) All of these

188. Homogenous group of sampling is an example of_______ sampling.

a) Cluster
b) Systematic
c) Deliberate
d) None

189. The purpose of research may broadly be grouped into _______ categories.

a) 2
b) 3
c) 4
d) 5

190. Concepts like ______ are examples of variables.
a) Weight
b) Height
c) Income
d) All of these

191. In which data we cannot do anything except set up inequalities?
a) Interval data
b) Ordinal data
c) Nominal data
d) Ratio data

192. Large group of sample is controlled by ______.
a) Matching
b) Elimination and matching
c) Randomization
d) Elimination

193. Who determined the size of class interval?
a) H.Odum
b) Y.Young
c) H.A Sturges
d) A.L Bowleys

194. Ex post facto is the scientific study which systematically discovers relation and interaction among variables in real life situation such as ______.
a) Communities
b) Factories
c) Colleges
d) All

195. Cluster sampling is known as ______.
a) Multi-stage sampling
b) Secondary sampling
c) Primary sampling unit
d) Area sampling

196. In critically reviewing a report of a quantitative study the area of the report you would focus on to appraise credibility is the ______.
a) Introduction
b) Methodology
c) Ethical issues
d) Report of analysis

197. In which Non-Parametric Test, following formula is used? rho = 6" D/N (N-1)
a) Median test
b) Sign test
c) Chi square test
d) Rho correlation

198. ______ is defined as the study of a problem in a situation.
a) Field experiment
b) Laboratory experiment
c) Diagnostic studies
d) Descriptive studies

199. A concept which can take on different quantitative value is called ________.

a) Variable b) Extraneous variable

c) Experimental d) None

200. Which of the following refer to purpose of research design?

a) To provide answer to research question

b) To provide control variance

c) Both a & b

d) None of these

201. The different conditions under which experimental and control groups are put in usually referred to as___

a) Experimental b) Treatments

c) Extraneous variables d) Independent variables

202. The name of_______is associated with differential scale.

a) Rotham Sted b) Morg

c) Redmen d) L.L Thurstone

203. In its present usage, the word statistics is ______.

a) A century old b) Two centuries old

c) Five centuries old d) A decade old

204. _______ is characterized by a flexibility of approach to questioning.

a) Clinical interview b) Unstructured interview

c) Non directive interview d) Focused interview

205. _______ is considered as the heart of the survey operation.

a) General form b) Question sequence

c) Question formulation d) Questionnaire

206. Which of the following comes under the examples of independent variables?

a) Ready made films b) Lecturer

c) Both a & b d) Environmental manipulation

207. Which of the following is negative correlation?

a) Poor working condition retards output

b) Corruption in India is increasing

c) Poor intelligence means poor achievement in school

d) An increase in population will lead to a short age of food grains

208. Entire data may be divided into a number of groups or classes or usually called _______.

a) Class intervals b) Class magnitude

c) Statistics of variables d) Statistics of attributes

209. _______ helps those interested in further research and studying the problem from another angle.

a) Bibliography b) Schedule

c) Both a & b d) None

210. Which of the following is classified under survey research?

a) Personal interview b) Mail questionnaire

c) Telephone survey d) All of these

211. What is the aim of grounded-theory analysis techniques?

a) To ensure that researchers report accurately trends in the data and different aspects of the data

b) To ensure that researchers produce results that are inline with current theory.

c) To ensure that researchers enter into intimate contact with their data and bring it in-line with current theory.

d) To ensure that researchers enter into intimate contact with their data and bring into juxtaposition different aspects of the data

212. In experimental research variables are classified into

a) Dependent and independent b) Continuous and dependent

c) Independent d) Broken and independent

213. The one variable about which the experimenter makes a prediction

a) Independent b) Dependent

c) Continuous d) All of the above

214. It is the spread between the highest and the lowest score

a) Standard deviation b) Range

c) Ratio d) None

215. Measure of variation is useful because

a) Tells us how representative the average is

b) Provides a yardstick on how much variability

c) Gives representative value

d) All

216. Secondary data can be obtained from

a) Journals, reports b) Govt & private publications

c) Trade d) All

217. Secondary data should be used with utmost care because of

a) Existing errors, bias b) Inadequate sample

c) Substitution d) All

218. Which aspects should investigator examine in using secondary data

a) Suitability b) Adequacy

c) Both a and b d) Interest

219. After the data has been edited the next step is to

a) Computerize it b) Publish it

c) Classify it d) None

220. Data to be analyzed is presented in the form of

1. Bar charts 2. Graphic

3. Tabular 4. Pictorial presentation

a) 1,2,3,4 b) 1,2,3

c) 1,2 d) 1,4

221. Out of some generalizations some conclusions are drawn in _______

a) Deductive method b) Inductive method

c) Both a and b d) None

222. Some facts are collected from which some conclusions in the broader and wider sense are drawn in ________

a) Deductive method b) Inductive method
c) Both a and b d) None

223. Each data entered in Z^2 test is known as

a) Row b) Column
c) Cell d) None

224. If a business woman orders a market survey to be conducted for her product, the report submitted must be ________

a) Elaborate b) Simple
c) Non-technical d) None

225. The Research report means ____________

a) Small research coordinated b) Small research consolidated
c) One single theory d) All of these

226. The purpose of the report is _________.

a) Dissipation of knowledge b) Broadcasting of generalizations
c) Widest use in public d) All of these

227. The standard deviation of sampling distribution is called _______.

a) Sampling error b) Size of sample
c) Both a and b d) Standard error

228. The survey is sometimes conducted at the instance of a third party that has some stake in the problem such surveys deal with

a) Market research
b) Market poll
c) Results not meant for general public
d) All

229. A report may be technical but it cannot afford to be

a) Incomplete b) Ambiguous
c) Sweeping remarks d) All

230. While editing primary data which of the following need attention

1. Data should be complete
2. Data should be consistent
3. Data should be adequate
4. Data should be homogenous

a) 1,2,3,4
b) 1,2,3
c) 1,2,
d) 1,4

231. Which of the following is the main source of case data?

a) Diaries
b) Autobiography
c) Letter
d) All of these

232. ______ represents the actual amount of variables.

a) Nominal scale
b) Ordinal scale
c) Ratio scale
d) Interval scale

233. ______ scale is also known as numerical scale.

a) Itemized rating scale
b) Ratio scale
c) Nominal scale
d) Ordinal scale

234. List containing all sampling units is known as ______.

a) Sampling design
b) Sampling frame
c) Sampling techniques
d) Sampling units

235. Case data are quite useful for ________.

a) Diagnosis
b) Therapy
c) Practical case problems
d) All of these

236. Which of the below data sources is most appropriate for grounded-theory analysis?

a) A structured interview
b) Self-report questionnaires
c) An unstructured focus group transcription
d) All of these

237. At what stage is the literature review completed when doing grounded-theory analysis?

a) After data collection, but before coding, to aid the coding process.
b) After coding but before categorization, to aid the labeling of categories
c) Lastly, in order to prevent analysis becoming theory driven
d) At the beginning of the research process in order to aid the formulation of ideas and hypotheses

238. Semantic differential scale is developed by ______.

a) Charles b) Osgood

c) G.J Suci d) P.H Tannenbaum

239. Scientific knowledge is example of ______.

a) Laboratory b) Field

c) Both a & b d) None

240. The pre determined plots or the blocks of different treatment are called ______.

a) Experimental unit b) Experiment

c) Confounded relationship d) None of these

241. ______ is also known as the product moment correlation coefficient.

a) Charles Spearman's Coefficient of Correlation

b) Karl Pearson's Coefficient of Correlation

c) Coefficient of Standard Deviation

d) Coefficient of Variables

242. Which of the following is essential for good questionnaire?

a) Questionnaire should be comparatively short and simple

b) Size of the questionnaire should be kept in the minimum

c) Questions should proceed in logical sequence

d) All of these

243. Probability of a head and a tail of tossing four coins simultaneously is ______.

a) 1/3 b) 1/8

c) 1/4 d) 1/16

244. A critical review aims to ______.

a) Summaries information on a topic from all relevant literature to inform practice

b) Identify strengths and limitations to make conclusions about quality of the evidence

c) Identify weaknesses in research studies to make judgments' about their suitability

d) Describe the methods used to gain evidence in the research studies

245. Constraints or problems in a study are known as ________.

a) Assumption b) Generalization
c) Concepts d) Limitation

246. A ten year old child is taller than 8 years old ones is an example of ________.

a) Experimental studies b) Case studies
c) Cross-sectional studies d) Vertical studies

247. Who is the father of scientific social survey?

a) Y. Young b) Darwin
c) A.L Bowleys d) Best

248. The final paper of a critical review of literature contains ________.

a) A summary of each author's work you have read
b) A description of the findings in each piece of research
c) A synthesis of the analysis of the information in the reviewed papers
d) Your analysis of each piece of literature

249. The difference between the two class limits is known as ________.

a) Class magnitude b) Class intervals
c) Class limit d) Class variables

250. Final result of a study will be more accurate if the sample drawn is __.

a) Purposive
b) Representation of the population
c) Fixed by quota
d) Taken randomly

Answers

1. c 2. a 3. d 4. a 5. b 6. c 7. b 8. d 9. a 10. d
11. a 12. a 13. a 14. d 15. b 16. b 17. d 18. a 19. a 20. a
21. c 22. d 23. a 24. d 25. c 26. a 27. a 28. c 29. a 30. d
31. b 32. a 33. d 34. d 35. b 36. c 37. c 38. d 39. d 40. a
41. d 42. c 43. a 44. b 45. d 46. d 47. d 48. b 49. a 50. c

51. b	52. d	53. a	54. b	55. a	56. b	57. a	58. a	59. b	60. c
61. a	62. a	63. c	64. c	65. a	66. d	67. c	68. d	69. a	70. a
71. a	72. a	73. a	74. c	75. d	76. b	77. a	78. b	79. d	80. c
81. a	82. c	83. a	84. b	85. a	86. c	87. b	88. b	89. a	90. d
91. b	92. c	93. d	94. b	95. d	96. d	97. d	98. a	99. b	100. d
101. d	102. d	103. a	104. d	105. d	106. d	107. d	108. d	109. d	110. a
111. d	112. d	113. d	114. d	115. a	116. a	117. d	118. c	119. b	120. c
121. c	122. d	123. c	124. d	125. b	126. d	127. d	128. d	129. b	130. b
131. b	132. b	133. d	134. b	135. a	136. b	137. b	138. b	139. d	140. d
141. b	142. a	143. b	144. b	145. a	146. b	147. b	148. a	149. d	150. b
151. a	152. b	153. b	154. b	155. a	156. d	157. a	158. b	159. b	160. a
161. b	162. d	163. c	164. a	165. d	166. d	167. c	168. a	169. c	170. c
171. d	172. c	173. a	174. d	175. a	176. d	177. b	178. c	179. d	180. b
181. d	182. c	183. a	184. a	185. a	186. c	187. d	188. a	189. c	190. d
191. b	192. c	193. c	194. d	195. d	196. d	197. d	198. b	199. a	200. c
201. b	202. d	203. a	204. b	205. d	206. c	207. d	208. a	209. a	210. d
211. d	212. a	213. b	214. b	215. d	216. d	217. d	218. c	219. c	220. a
221. a	222. b	223. c	224. c	225. d	226. d	227. d	228. d	229. d	230. a
231. d	232. c	233. a	234. b	235. d	236. c	237. c	238. d	239. c	240. a
241. b	242. d	243. d	244. d	245. c	246. c	247. d	248. b	249. a	250. b

□□□

References

1. Srilakshmi, B. (1996). Food Science, New Age International (P) Limited Publishers, New Delhi.
2. Srilakshmi, B. (1999). Dietetics, New Age International (P) Limited Publishers, New Delhi.
3. Srilakshmi, B. (2002). Nutrition Science, New Age International (P) Limited Publishers, New Delhi.
4. Vidyasagar, P.V. (1998). Handbook of Textiles, Mittal Publications, New Delhi.
5. Mullick, P. (1995). Textbook of Home Science.Kalyani Publishers, New Delhi.
6. Deacon, R.E. and Firebaugh, F.M. (1975). Home Management : Context and Concepts. Houghton, Mifflin Company, U.S.A.
7. Devadas, R.P. and Jaya, N. (1984).A Textbook on Child Development, Macmillan India Limited, New Delhi.
8. Sethi, M and Malhan, S. (1987). Catering Management, Wiley Eastern Limited, New Delhi.
9. Reddy, A.A. (1976). Extension Education , Sree Lakshmi Press, Baptala, Andhra Pradesh.

UNIVERSITY GRANTS COMMISSION
NET BUREAU

Code No. : 12

Subject : HOME SCIENCE

SYLLABUS AND SAMPLE QUESTIONS

Note :

There will be two question papers, Paper–II and Paper–III (Part–A & B). Paper–II will cover 50 Objective Type Questions (Multiple choice, Matching type, True/False, Assertion-Reasoning type) carrying 100 marks. Paper–II will have two Parts–A and B; Paper–III(A) will have 10 short essay-type questions (300 words) carrying 16 marks each. In it there will be one question with internal choice from each unit (i.e., 10 questions from 10 units; Total marks will be 160). Paper–III(B) will be compulsory and there will be one question from each of the Electives. The candidate will attempt only one question (one elective only in 800 words) carrying 40 marks. Total marks of Paper–III will be 200.

PAPER–II & PAPER–III(A) [CORE GROUP]

Unit—I : Food Science

- **Food Groups**
- **Food Preparation**
- **Food Preservation**
- **Food Science and Food Analysis**
- **Food Processing**

Unit—II : Nutrition Science

- **Fundamentals of nutrition**
- **Nutritional biochemistry**
- **Food microbiology**
- **Public nutrition**
- **Therapeutic nutrition**

Unit—III : Institutional Management

Management of Hospitality Institutes—Hospital/Hotel/Restaurant/Café and Outdoor catering

Management of Social Institutes—family as Institute, child care and Geriatric institutes, Panchayats